HOLY SPIRIT,
Make Your Home in Me

Biblical Meditations on Receiving the
Gift of the Spirit

D0211439

HOLY SPIRIT,
Make Your Home in Me

Biblical Meditations on Receiving
the Gift of the Spirit

George T. Montague, SM

The Word Among Us Press
7115 Guilford Drive
Frederick, Maryland 21704
www.wau.org

17 16 15 14 13   6 7 8 9 10
ISBN: 978-1-59325-128-4
eISBN: 978-1-59325-407-0

Scriptural translations are the author's own.

Edwin Hatch, "Breathe on Me, Breath of God," adapted by Anthony G. Petti. Copyright © 1971 by Faber Music Ltd. Reprinted from *New Catholic Hymnal* by kind permission of the publishers.

Cover design by John Hamilton

Made and printed in the United States of America

Library of Congress Cataloging-in-Publication Data
Montague, George T.
    Holy Spirit, make your home in me : biblical meditations on receiving the gift of the Spirit / George T. Montague.
        p. cm.
    ISBN 978-1-59325-128-4 (alk. paper)
  1. Baptism in the Holy Spirit--Meditations. 2. Pentecostalism--Catholic Church--Meditations. 3. Baptism in the Holy Spirit--Biblical teaching.
4. Bible--Meditations. 5. Baptism in the Holy Spirit--Biblical teaching.
I. Title.
  BX2350.57.M66 2008
  234'.13--dc22
                                    2007047555

Contents

Introduction

Invitation

Let the one who thirsts come forward, the one who wishes it come forward and receive the gift of life-giving water.
—Revelation 22:17

On Christmas Eve 1970, something dramatic and life changing happened to me. For several weeks, I had been attending a prayer meeting at St. Mary's University in San Antonio, Texas. I had been drawn to it because I was thirsting in my spiritual life. Was it a middle-age crisis or the noonday devil? Maybe a mixture of both, but something was missing in my life. I had been a vowed religious for twenty-three years, an ordained priest for twelve years, and a teacher of theology for ten years. You would think that if anyone would be flying high spiritually, it would be me. But I had experienced emotional burnout two years earlier; and although I had recovered fairly well, there was a restlessness in my soul that cried out, "My God, I need something!"

The prayer meeting was addressing that need, but in a way that was challenging. The participants, who numbered in the hundreds, seemed to enjoy nothing more than praising God with uplifted hands and strange tongues, and praying for healing for those asking for it. Many testified about the wonders God had done in their lives, and they attributed the beginning of it to "the baptism in the Holy Spirit." All this was very new and strange to me. I was trying to run it all through my theological categories. That sort of repetitive, almost ecstatic praise is exactly what I read every day in the psalms. And the psalmist often said he lifted up his hands in prayer. Tongues was one of the ways people prayed in the New Testament, and like Jesus, they healed people. So the problem was not really my theological categories but my resistance to letting other people pray over me, which is what they said this baptism in the Holy Spirit involved. I was attached to my image. I was the spiritual authority! Why did I need other people to pray over me? After all, I had been prayed over and anointed by a bishop!

And yet I could not deny my thirst. So finally I yielded, knelt down, and asked for the gift of the Holy Spirit through the prayer of simple lay people. I knew it would not be the first time I had received the Holy Spirit. As a Catholic, I had been baptized in infancy, confirmed as a teenager, called to religious life, and ordained a priest. But I also knew that the grace of those past markings on my soul had not yet taken over my life, and what I saw in the lay people was like the Lord saying to me, "George, I have more for you. Will you let me give it to you? It will take an act of humility on your part. But I invite you to join with all the Zacchaeuses who have climbed a tree to see me. And see me you will."

It was a new beginning. I can understand why some of my Christian brothers and sisters call it a "born again" experience, though we Catholics prefer to reserve that description for the Sacrament of Baptism. A new spiritual energy burst up from within me, and I experienced the reality of what Jesus said to the Samaritan woman: "The water I will give him will become a fountain of water springing up to eternal life" (John 4:14). My life and my ministry thereafter became alive in a way they never had been before. Not that I had attained perfection, God forbid! But I experienced a new energy to run where before I had only walked, to sing where before I had only spoken.

And when, thirty-seven years later, Bert Ghezzi of The Word Among Us Press invited me to write a book on receiving the Holy Spirit, I did not hesitate for very long. Here was a chance to weave my long experience of the Holy Spirit with biblical reflections that have grown on me through prayer and study. This book is not really a formal biblical study. The method of the Fathers of the church has inspired me, without, of course, obliging me to follow their excessive allegorizing. This book is a series of meditations or homilies, if you will, leading to a prayer at the end of each chapter. It is for those of any status or of any age in the spiritual life, whether you have received the baptism in the Holy Spirit or have not. If you have received it or in any other way experienced an outpouring of the Holy Spirit in your life, I hope these pages will help you grow further. If you have the kind of primary thirst I had, these meditations may whet your thirst even more, and maybe the Holy Spirit will even fall upon you as you read.

George T. Montague, SM

Chapter I

Gift

It was homily time. Not for the usual parish congregation, but for my extended family and friends gathered at our ancestral home for a Mass anticipating Christmas.

"It's a feast for children," I began, "and so I'm looking for help." On this annual occasion, I always invited the youngest child capable of speech to sit beside me and assist me in exploring the mystery of Christmas.

All eyes turned on Rachel, my four-year-old grandniece, who, after considerable prodding, shyly and with great reluctance inched forward and sat beside me.

"Rachel, what is Christmas all about?"

No answer. I'd better give her some help.

"Is it about the birthday of Jesus?"

A nod but not a word.

"And what do we do at Christmas?"

No answer.

"Do we give gifts?"

Another nod, this time more vigorous. But still no word.

"And what do you do when you get a gift?" I could hear a wave of whispers from the adults coaching her: "You say thanks. You say thanks." But Rachel would hear none of it. She gave me a look as if I had asked a really stupid question, and blurted out, "You open it!"

This book is about a gift that for many of us still lies unopened. It was unopened for me until I was forty-one years old and knelt down and asked some friends to pray over me for the baptism in the Holy Spirit. Oh sure, I had been baptized and confirmed. I had professed religious vows, and I had been ordained twelve years earlier. And surely the Holy Spirit had been at work in those moments. But what happened on that Christmas Eve in 1970 was such a breakthrough, such an explosion of spiritual energy, that I felt I had never really known the Holy Spirit before then. As the old African-American spiritual says, "We didn't know who you was." It was the discovery of a lifetime.

I've written my personal testimony elsewhere. And in other books, I've explored as with an archeologist's trowel the Scripture passages dealing with the Holy Spirit. But here I invite you to walk with me as, putting technicalities aside, I seek to open the gift of the Holy Spirit as he comes to us in the wrapping of the word.

The Gift of the Person

Necklaces, sweaters, iPods, cars—what do all these have in common? They can be gifts. Christmas, birthdays, and weddings call for gifts. When we think of gifts, most of the time we think of material things—even at weddings, where we celebrate the most important exchange of gifts that happens before our very eyes—the gift of two persons to each other. The total gift of self is most obvious at weddings, where we celebrate promises made, and at anniversaries, where we celebrate promises kept. But there are other ways persons give themselves totally. My brother Charlie died on the sands of a South Pacific island in World War II. Like thousands of others, he gave his life to defend his family, his friends, his country—and his bride-to-be back home. She, too, though having no choice, shared in her own way that higher gift of self. Unable to give herself totally to him in life, she was one with him in his self-gift for his country. Those who embrace celibacy for the kingdom do so as a direct gift to God and to his people. It is a mystery that the ultimate fulfillment of ourselves happens when we give ourselves away. Thus the joy when people realize that they themselves are the perfect gift.

But what about Rachel's "You open it"? Does this apply to persons as well as to things? If we reflect for a moment, we will see that it is true—except that it is the Gift, rather than the receiver, who does the opening. Little by little, the married person reveals the depths of his or her being to the other. And the other receives the revelation as a further gift, freely reciprocating with the gift of growing openness. And so it happens in less intense ways, perhaps, in other forms of personal commitment.

When we as human beings give, we only give what we have been given. For what do we have that we have not received (1 Corinthians 4:7)? From whom do we first receive? Ultimately, from the Giver of all, God. Look about you. Everything you see has been given to you and to the world by God. Do you think of it that way? It is a grace already to see creation as his gift. Reason itself tells us that there must be a first cause for what just *is* before us. But to see it with a reverential heart—that is a grace. And there are many in the world, even among those who have a very vague notion of a supreme being, who reverence creation that way. They have a sense that creation is a gift.

As our brother Jews say at their Seder meals, if we knew God only through creation, that would be enough. But we know that this God, the Creator, wanted more for us. Not only did he create us with an intelligence and free will, thus making us more like himself than any of the rest of creation, he also wanted to enter into a personal relationship with us. How did he do it? Not by the material world he gave us. Not even by the experience of personal self-giving on the human level, which is but a shadow of his person. He decided to *give himself to us*.

A Shared Communion

Have you ever given someone a present that they did not appreciate, or maybe even rejected? Given the fact that his first offer to Adam and Eve had been rejected, plunging the human race into a landslide of evil, the Lord wanted to make sure that at least some would accept this gift of himself. So he entered into a long pedagogy with his chosen people, leading them through Abraham and Moses and the prophets and the often painful events of their history to prepare a heart ready to receive him. He found the perfect heart, not in the multitude, but in a single young woman, Mary of Nazareth. There, in giving himself to her, he gave himself in person to the whole human race. The story of the annunciation, told by the inspired pen of Luke, reveals a God who is indeed one but also three: the Father who begot his eternal Son in time and the Holy Spirit who worked this miracle. We learn that God is not solitary. God is communion. And now that communion is shared with the human race in a way beyond what the human heart could imagine (1 Corinthians 2:9-10): the Son of God in the fleshly womb of a woman is the supreme communication of a personal God to the human race.

The New Testament authors revel in telling of the gift of the Son. "God so loved the world that he *gave* his only Son, that whoever believes in him might not perish but might have eternal life" (John 3:16). "He loved me and *gave* himself up for me" (Galatians 2:20). God the Father gave his Son to Mary and through her to us. Then the Son gave himself up *for* us, that we might live. It was infinitely more than my brother's dying so that his wife-to-be (and the rest of us Americans) might live. It was the divine Bridegroom's dying so that his bride-to-be, the church, might live. And in the person of Mary at the foot of the cross, the bride/mother-to-be, the new Eve beside the new Adam, agonized with the dying Spouse. The yes of the new Adam and the yes of the new Eve reversed the curse of Eden and reopened paradise. (The Bible does not hesitate to mix figures and symbols when dealing with mystery.)

But all this happened before we were born—indeed, before anyone other than Mary and the first disciples said yes to God's plan. And even for those first disciples, the full meaning of what happened on Good Friday and Easter Sunday escaped them at the moment it was happening. Jesus knew that it would be so. Thus, he promised them the Holy Spirit, so that the external, objective act of redemption might become the internal experience of the believer. To the woman at the well of Samaria, Jesus said, "If you knew the *gift of God* and who it is that is speaking with you, you might have asked him and he would have *given* you living water" (John 4:10). Later in the Gospel of John, Jesus said that the living water is the Holy Spirit (John 7:37-39). In Luke's gospel, Jesus said, "If you . . . know how to give good gifts to your children, how much more will the heavenly Father *give* the Holy Spirit to those who ask him!" (Luke 11:13). At the first Christian Pentecost, at the end of Peter's sermon, the bystanders asked, "What are we to do?" (Acts 2:37). Peter responded, "Repent and be baptized, each one of you, in the name of Jesus, the Messiah, for the forgiveness of your sins, and you will receive the *gift* of the Holy Spirit" (2:38).

So the gift is not only Jesus in person, it is also the Spirit of Jesus in person. But there is more, and we find a key to that "more" in the first letter we have from Paul, written about A.D. 51. Counseling the Thessalonians sternly about sexual morality, he wrote, "Whoever disregards this, disregards not a human being but God, who *is giving* his Holy Spirit to you" (1 Thessalonians 4:8). I have italicized "is giving" because the present tense opens up another marvelous facet of this Gift. The Holy Spirit is given by the Father and the Son not only at the moment of Baptism. The Holy Spirit is not a gift that just sits there. The Holy Spirit is being given at every moment by the Father and the Son. We know from elsewhere that the Spirit flows from the Father and the Son, for the Holy Spirit is the river of life-giving water flowing from the throne of God and the Lamb (Revelation 22:1). This is what we mean when we say in the Creed, "I believe in the Holy Spirit, who proceeds from the Father and the Son." If you are in communion with Jesus—or what is called the state of grace—God the Father and God the Son are pouring forth their love as the Holy Spirit in your heart right now. You have a divine Niagara Falls flowing in you at this very moment. In you, the Father is loving the Son, the Son is loving the Father, and Father and Son are giving you their mutual love in the Holy Spirit.

Yes, their mutual love. It is already a great grace to know that God is love. That would be true if we knew God only as the one God, creator and caller of his chosen people of old. But by the gift of the Holy Spirit, we are caught up in the mutual interpersonal love of the holy Trinity. Through the revelation of Jesus, we know that God is a communion of persons. The awesome, unspeakable gift is that by the Holy Spirit we are drawn into the mutual embrace of Father and Son. I once photographed a father and mother simultaneously kissing their eighteen-month-old son on opposite cheeks. That, I thought, is what the Father and Jesus are doing to us, and their kiss is the Holy Spirit. And unless we pull away from it, the kissing never stops!

It is by faith that we know these wonders to be true. But how does that truth become a transforming experience for us? It is the same Holy Spirit who will achieve the transformation if we sincerely seek him in prayer. The good news is that God wants to give us the Holy Spirit more than we want to receive him. "If you, who are evil, know how to give good gifts to your children, how much more will the heavenly Father give the Holy Spirit to those who ask him!" (Luke 11:13).

....

Come, Holy Spirit. You who are Love, the fire of the Father and the Son's mutual love, the cause and source of all other loves, reveal yourself to me. Although I am unworthy to receive the gift of yourself, my very

17

unworthiness shows how much your love is an unmerited gift. In giving me yourself, you will also show me the face of the Father and the Son, and I will know myself as son/daughter of the Father and brother/sister of the Son. Amen.

Chapter 2

"But How Can This Be?"

There are two problems with realizing the dream described in the previous chapter. One is that we are creatures. The other is that we are sinners, unworthy of such a gift.

Is it really possible that the infinite God could meet me, a finite creature, in a real, living, personal self-giving relationship? Friendship, after all, is between equals, and there is an infinite distance between God and me. It's good once in a while to think about the meaning of infinity. I grew up in Texas, where "the stars at night are big and bright." Many a summer night, I lay out in the yard of our ranch home and marveled at the array. Only later did I learn that I was seeing the light that left those stars eons before I was born. In the 1990s, astronomers caught sight of a supernova, an exploding star whose light finally reached the earth. The light of that explosion, traveling at the speed of 186,000 miles a second, took 160,000 light years to reach the earth. The scientists were seeing something that happened 160,000 years ago! And even that is not infinity.

While visiting the Grand Canyon with my family, I sat one evening on the canyon's edge as the twilight began to welcome the stars. The canyon's river was a mile below me. There was no limit to the horizons around me or to the sky above me. For an instant I panicked, feeling like a grain of sand being swallowed up by infinity.

Spirit, Soul, and Body

The awesomeness of creation and the Creator is so overwhelming to Muslims that it is the foundation, the only foundation of their faith. Muslims relate to Allah only as Creator, not as Father and friend. The distance is too great to think otherwise. There is nothing in the human being that could receive God in any other way. But Christians have a different understanding of God and of the otherwise unthinkable possibility of a personal encounter with him, should God so choose. When St. Paul prayed for his disciples in Thessalonica, he wrote, "May the God of peace make you holy through and through, and may your whole being, spirit, soul, and body, be preserved blameless for the coming of our Lord Jesus Christ" (1 Thessalonians 5:23). "Spirit, soul, and body" make up our "whole being." St. Paul was probably thinking of the story of the creation of Adam in Genesis 2:7, where God took clay and breathed into it the breath of life, and man became a living soul. The three elements are there: body from the soil, the breath of God as spirit, and soul as the resultant principle of human life. As you may have already guessed, "spirit" will be the key to understanding how we human beings can receive the person of God. But to understand ourselves fully, we must first look at the other two elements, body and soul.

In Paul's thought, "body" relates us to all material creation, to all that is lumpy, space taking, and collision prone. The human being in the creation story in Genesis 2 is *adam* from *adamah*, earth man from earth. God took mud and fashioned man from it. So I am brother or sister to the stars, the flowers, even the ants—as St. Francis lyrically sang. "Body" suggests solidarity not only with the earth and material creation but also with other human beings (each of them is a body), especially those who are suffering. "Think of those in prison as yourselves in prison with them, and those enduring suffering as dwelling yourselves in the body" (Hebrews 13:3). The parallelism we would expect in the second half of that sentence would read, "as suffering with them," but it reads, "as dwelling yourselves in the body." So is it any wonder that when Paul wanted to show our union, our solidarity in Christ, he would say, "You are Christ's body" (1 Corinthians 12:27)? The church's whole sacramental system is built on our "bodiliness"—water, oil, bread, touch become channels of the touch of God.

But we are not just body. Like a tree that, rooted in the earth, organizes its life via the trunk, we, too, have a principle of organization that we call "the soul." Created directly by God, it makes the difference between us and other bodies in the universe. It enables us to think, to organize our experience, to remember, to create tools and works of art, to master and care for the world. We can understand and can choose freely what we want to do. Because we can communicate and receive communication, we can also hear the word of God.

The highest principle within us, Paul said (he listed it first), is our spirit. Again, like the tree that reaches its height by spreading out its limbs to receive the rain and the sun, our spirit is that part of us that reaches beyond ourselves to the transcendent.

It is our receptor. As our outstretched arms beckon infinity, so the spirit beckons what our body and our mind cannot contain. And that means we have a capacity for God. A capacity is a potential. It doesn't mean the contact has happened. Nor does it mean that we would completely comprehend God if the contact did happen. But it does mean that we have not only the capacity but also a basic drive to make that contact, just as the tree hungers for rain and sun without being able to produce either. As St. Augustine prayed, "You have made us for yourself, O Lord, and we are restless until we rest in you."

Our Spirit Meets God's Spirit

It is precisely here, in our spirit, that God's Holy Spirit comes to meet us. "The Holy Spirit bears united witness with our spirit that we are the children of God" (Romans 8:16). Because we are spirit and God is spirit, the awesome connection can be made. It begins with God's initiative and God's choice, but we have to be open to receive. We must want to receive, for the Spirit will be given to those who ask: "If you . . . know how to give good gifts to your children, how much more will the Father in heaven give the Holy Spirit to those who ask him!" (Luke 11:13). That assumes, of course, that we have at least a glimpse of what we are asking for. If, like the disciples of John the Baptist at Ephesus, "we have not even heard that there is a Holy Spirit" (Acts 19:2), then we won't even know to ask. Now, while many Christians may have heard the term "Holy Spirit" and may have even said many times in the Creed, "I believe in the Holy Spirit," they may never really have understood the Gift, because they have not experienced him. One of the purposes of this book is to tell more about him, with the hope of creating an ardent desire and prayer for that encounter. And even if we have had some experience of the Holy Spirit already, perhaps at a retreat or in prayer, we can never exhaust the Gift, because one of the ways you can spell the name of God is M-O-R-E, infinitely MORE.

The problem, then, for receiving the Holy Spirit is not an incapacity on our part. The real problem is sin. If our spirit is capable of receiving the Spirit of God, if our mind is capable of receiving his word, if our body is capable of receiving his healing and even receiving the body of the Lord in the Eucharist, it is also possible that each of these dimensions can block the Holy Spirit because of the infection of sin. For example, our body, which is made to glorify God (1 Corinthians 6:20), can be dominated by the flesh. Our mind can be fogged by half-truths that we indulge in to justify our sinful behavior. And, worst of all, our spirit can be opened to evil spirits if we begin to dabble in the occult and experiment with palm or tarot-card readers, astrology, Ouija boards, séances, and so forth.

Repentance

If we are infected by sin of any kind, can we still receive the Holy Spirit? Yes, but on one condition: repentance. The Wisdom of Solomon tells us that the holy spirit of discipline flees deceit and sin (1:4-5). But that is not the end of the story. To those on the first Pentecost who asked what they should do to receive the Holy Spirit, Peter said, "*Repent* and be baptized, every one of you, in the name of Jesus Christ for the forgiveness of your sins, and you will receive the gift of the Holy Spirit" (Acts 2:38). Jesus began his ministry with the same message: "*Repent*, for the kingdom of heaven is at hand" (Matthew 3:2). To experience the kingdom here and now, to experience the power of the Holy Spirit, the way is simple, if at times difficult: repent.

Repentance is particularly difficult, not only for entrenched sinners but also for religious people who think they have no need of repentance. Such was the case of the Pharisee who told God how proud he should be that his servant fasted twice a week, gave tithes, and did everything by the book (Luke 18:9-14). He didn't need anything more, unlike the tax collector who beat his breast and said, "God, be merciful to me, a sinner." Jesus began his Sermon on the Mount not with a series of do's and don'ts, nor with a praise of the righteous. He began by saying how blessed are those who are broken in spirit, those who are mourning, those who know they need something, those who know they need God. The Pharisees as portrayed in the gospels were "good" people, externally at least, but they lacked one thing: an openness to the God who had MORE for them.

One day when the disciples asked Jesus who was the greatest in the kingdom, he placed a little child in their midst and told them that unless they became like little children, they wouldn't even get into the kingdom, much less be the greatest: "Unless you turn . . ." (Matthew 18:1-4). The conversion he was talking about here was not a conversion from a life of great sin, but a conversion to spiritual childhood. Children may have lots of faults, but if you give a child a gift, he will take it. That was the problem with the Pharisees. Jesus offered them a gift, but they would not receive it. For them, the "better" was a threat to the "good."

That can happen in our lives, too. We may not be living in a spiritual gutter, but we may be on a spiritual plateau. We may be quite satisfied with where we are, a bit like the people of Laodicea, who said they were rich and needed nothing but didn't realize that they were the wretched and poor and blind and naked ones (Revelation 3:17). That attitude can be even more dangerous than obvious sin, since it has virtue as its veneer but tepidity at its core. The Christian life is a journey, not a retirement center.

If our blockage is not self-satisfaction and tepidity, it may be just the opposite: the conviction that we are not worthy. Who am I to receive such a wondrous gift? Just asking that question shows how such an attitude assumes that we have to earn the Holy Spirit. But the Holy Spirit is not a reward. The Holy Spirit is Gift. As Jesus came not to save the righteous but sinners (Matthew 9:13), so the Holy Spirit does not want anyone to be a prisoner of his or her past. No matter how wretched our personal histories have been, God wants to make us new creations (2 Corinthians 5:17). We just have to be willing to believe that he can, and then let him do it. Don't pretend that you are your own god and judge yourself unworthy. If the Son of God bought you with his own blood, you must be worth something! You are the pearl of great price for which the divine Merchant sold all he had so he could have you (Matthew 13:45-46).

Another blockage is a fear of losing control. We often measure our maturity and our importance by our ability to control. We speak of mastering mathematics, mastering a language, mastering the computer. The ability to do so is a gift, and it corresponds to God's plan for humanity to have dominion over the earth (Genesis 1:28). But this tendency can sometimes block our growth if it is time to let go of something we are trying to control but can't. "Lord, give me the serenity to accept the things I cannot change, the courage to change the things I can, and the wisdom to know the difference." Rowing can be an enjoyable exercise for a time, but there comes a time when we rest the oars and lift the sail. That's what happens when we yield to the Holy Spirit. And sometimes it takes an external act of humility (like Zacchaeus climbing a tree or someone yielding to the gift of tongues) to really let go—as it did for me when I finally knelt down and asked some lay people to pray for the release of the Holy Spirit in me.

....

Father, creator of heaven and earth and creator of me, I am overwhelmed by the thought that you, the infinite God, could reveal the inner mystery of your being to me, a speck of dust in the vast universe. I thank you, however, for creating me not just body and soul but also spirit, whereby I could become one with you through your Holy Spirit. I repent of my sins, and I open the remnants of my woundedness to your healing love and mercy. I ask you for a new outpouring of your Holy Spirit, that I may know you and your Son, Jesus, in a way I've never known before. Amen.

Chapter 3

Life-Breath

At the age of five, my grandnephew Charlie was already a seasoned cowboy. But even seasoned cowboys can sometimes get thrown from a horse, especially if the rider is caught off balance when the horse "spooks"—cowboy language for a sudden rearing or sideward lunge when something scares the horse. The ride was over and Charlie was ready to dismount, when Sundance spooked, landing Charlie on the ground beneath the hind legs of the half-ton animal. A hoof slammed down on his skull. Blood shot from Charlie's nostrils and ears, and his little body turned limp and breathless. His father sped to his side and began blowing into his mouth. A three-minute eternity passed until Charlie at last regained his breath. Helicopter, emergency room, skilled doctors, and intense family prayer did the rest. Charlie went on to play football for his school. But life began again with his breath.

When I begin a talk on the Holy Spirit, I sometimes ask the members of the audience to hold their breath for as long as they can. As one by one they let go in this gentle contest, they are reminded how precious their breath is, and how utterly dependent upon it they are. To breathe is to live.

No doubt that is why God, wanting to tell us what his Holy Spirit is, chose our life-breath as a primal image. Already in the earliest pages of the Old Testament we see that image emerging. How does Genesis describe the creation of the first man? God blew into his nostrils the breath of life, and man became a living being (2:7). Other tribes and groups of people were aware that man was essentially different from the material world and the animals and that he belonged to a higher realm. In the Babylonian creation myth, man is made of clay mixed with the blood of the gods. But in the Genesis account, the combination is more spiritual—literally, because in Hebrew and in Greek, breath and spirit are closely related, sometimes even synonyms. God doesn't lose any blood; he doesn't even lose his breath when he gives it away. But if man is a living being, it is because God has given him the breath of life.

On the day of his resurrection, Jesus relived the Genesis story in a powerful, dramatic way. Appearing to his disciples, he first wished them peace, and then he breathed on them and said, "Receive the Holy Spirit" (John 20:19-22). Why did he use the gesture of breathing on them? He wanted to tell them that the church, taken from men who were still quite earthbound like Adam, was the beginning of a new humanity because Jesus was giving his own breath, the Holy Spirit, to fill them with his own divine life.

The Eternal Breath of God

Is it too much to think of the Holy Spirit as the breath of Jesus? The evangelist John didn't think so. For in describing the moment of Jesus' death on the cross, he didn't say that Jesus "breathed his last" (Mark 15:37; Luke 23:46) or "he gave up his spirit" (Matthew 27:50). Rather, John said, "He handed over the Spirit" (John 19:30). The fourth evangelist, who looked for deep, symbolic meaning in the events of Jesus' life, saw something more in this moment than just the end of Jesus' life. The last breath of Jesus was the first breath of the Spirit for the little community huddled at the foot of the cross. The Holy Spirit was given not merely through the resurrection of Jesus but also through the death of Jesus on the cross! If you are asking for the Holy Spirit, you are asking Jesus to breathe on you!

There is more here than meets the eye. Does Jesus' breath tell us something beyond the human drama played out in these gospel scenes? Does it reveal something about the inner mystery of God, the holy Trinity? Indeed it does. We know that the Holy Spirit proceeds from the Father and the Son. At the Last Supper, Jesus said that he would send the Holy Spirit who proceeds from the Father (John 15:26). And the same word, "proceed," is used in the Book of Revelation for the river of life-giving water flowing from God and the Lamb (Revelation 22:1). But we know that the Son also proceeds from the Father (John 17:8; 20:21). In the midst of debates about the Trinity, later church councils clarified how the proceeding of the Spirit differs from that of the Son. The Son, they defined, proceeds from the Father by way of generation, the Holy Spirit by way of the mutual *spiration* of the Father and the Son (Council of Florence, A.D. 1439). *Spiration* means breathing forth. The Father and the Son *breathe forth* the Holy Spirit. Think of two lovers breathing forth together their sigh of mutual love. That is what the Father and the Son are doing continually and eternally. Their one sigh of love is the person of the Holy Spirit.

When Jesus breathed the Spirit from the cross, when he breathed upon the disciples from his risen body, *and when he breathes on us*, he was—and is—doing in time what he does with the Father eternally in the intimate mystery of the Trinity. Jesus' breath is the eternal breath of God! Could anything more wonderful be imagined?

Face-to-Face with God

You can't breathe on someone unless you get close, and if the receiver's eyes are open, he or she will see your face. There are three places in the Old Testament where the Spirit and the face of God are joined. (The word "face" is often translated "presence" in our English bibles, but in the translations I give below I am sticking to the literal meaning of the Hebrew, "face.") In Psalm 139:7, where the psalmist is overwhelmed with God's presence everywhere, we read, "Where can I escape your *spirit?* From your *face* where can I flee?" The second instance is when the Lord promises to restore his people from their exile in Babylon and says, "No longer will I hide my *face* from them, for I have poured out my *spirit* on the house of Israel, says the LORD" (Ezekiel 39:29). The third instance, in Psalm 51, is the most important because the expression "*holy* spirit" appears. The psalmist, having confessed his sins and asked for God's cleansing, goes on to beg God to create in him a brand new heart, and then he says, "Do not cast me away from your *face,* and take not your *Holy Spirit* from me" (51:11). Although the psalmist did not know the person of the Holy Spirit as we do, we are justified now in rereading the text in the light of the Spirit's full revelation in the New Testament. If God is breathing his holy breath upon us, then we must be face-to-face with God!

But how does this square with what Scripture says elsewhere, that "we walk by faith and not by sight" (2 Corinthians 5:7), and that in this life we see obscurely and only in the next life face-to-face (1 Corinthians 13:12)? The solution is simple: God is breathing on us with our eyes closed. We live in the night of faith, but his face is close to us. We know his presence by his breath, and that is enough—for now.

Formerly, the rite of baptism in the Catholic Church included the gesture of the priest or deacon's breathing gently onto the baptized. Although this part of the ritual is no longer used, the symbolism remains, because baptism is the moment when the breath of God, the Holy Spirit, is breathed into the one baptized. A new creation is taking place. As God began the human race by breathing into Adam, he is starting over with the humanity of this child or adult to remake the world. Baptism has a cosmic dimension, which we will explore in a later chapter.

A glance back at the Old Testament will complete our picture of the Spirit as the breath of God. We have already seen how the very creation of the human race is an effect of God's breathing life into Adam. This is a prototype of God's breathing life into everything that lives (Psalm 150:6; see Acts 17:25). If God takes back the life-breath of anything, it dies (Psalm 104:29; Job 34:14). When Scripture says that God used his breath to create the heavens (Psalm 33:6) or to slay his enemies (2 Samuel 22:16; Job 4:9), it is contrasting the effortlessness of God's action with the enormity of its effects. God just breathed, and the stars were made; God just breathed, and his enemies were destroyed. Not only was there no match of strength, there was no struggle at all. So Ezekiel called on the Spirit to breathe on the dry bones, and they came together, grew flesh, and stood up, a mighty army (37:5-10). Amazingly, when Isaiah describes the coming Messiah, he says that this ideal King will do what elsewhere only God can do: slay the wicked with the breath of his mouth (11:4). The New Testament sees this prophecy fulfilled in Jesus (2 Thessalonians 2:8 and "the sword of his mouth," Revelation 1:16; 2:16; 19:15, 21). Again, Jesus does not need guns or tanks or rockets. His breath is sufficient to win the victory. So if we receive the Holy Spirit, the breath of Jesus, we also will know how to win an overwhelming victory, no matter what the odds (Romans 8:37).

The following hymn is offered in the church's Liturgy of the Hours:

> Breathe on me, breath of God,
> Fill me with life anew,
> That I may love the things you love,
> And do what you would do.

> Breathe on me, breath of God,
> Until my heart is pure,
> Until with you I have one will,
> To live and to endure.

> Breathe on me, breath of God,
> My soul with grace refine,
> Until this earthly part of me
> Glows with your fire divine.

Breathe on me, breath of God,
So I shall never die,
But live with you the perfect life
In your eternity.[1]

Take a quiet moment in prayer. In faith, see Jesus before you. Ask him to breathe on you the gift of the Holy Spirit.

Chapter 4

Wind

The little hound dog with the floppy ears seemed happy to greet us. In fact, he seemed to be a committee of one to welcome visitors to the cemetery in Medjugorje, the only place outside the church where the Communist government allowed people to gather. I was with a group of pilgrims with whom I had talked about the baptism in the Holy Spirit, and now we were going to pray that each of them would receive it. We gathered, and I preached a final exhortation for all to be open, like Mary and the disciples in the upper room, for the coming Holy Spirit. A gentle breeze had been caressing our cheeks, but when we began singing "Come, Holy Ghost, Creator blest, . . ." two things happened. Our little welcoming committee of one launched into his version of the song, and a blast of wind almost knocked me over.

We hadn't asked for a sign, but the Lord chose to give us a delightful one that reminded us of the mighty wind of that first Pentecost—and some of us thought, perhaps, that the little dog, who didn't know the words, was encouraging us to sing in tongues!

Wind as an image of the Spirit is as old as the Bible itself. The book opens with these words: "In the beginning God created the heavens and the earth. The earth was waste and void, darkness covered the abyss, and a mighty wind was blowing over the surface of the waters" (Genesis 1:1-2). You may be more familiar with the translation that reads, "The spirit of God was hovering over the waters." The difference in translations is based on the enigmatic Hebrew *ruah elohim*, which can be translated, "a wind of God," "a mighty wind," or "the S(s)pirit of God." *Elohim* can mean "God," or it can mean "something of godly proportions." Likewise, *ruah* can mean "wind" or "spirit." If it is translated "wind," it could be part of the chaos. If translated "spirit," it could mean God's preparation to speak his word and bring order and beauty out of the formless, chaotic abyss. For reasons I have detailed previously,[2] I am persuaded that the best translation is the traditional one, "the spirit of God." Looking back from the New Testament, we can think of the Holy Spirit, and so "Spirit" could be capitalized; but since the Old Testament writers did not yet have an understanding of the person of the Holy Spirit, I've chosen to leave it as they probably thought of it. But God intended it, I believe, to teach us ultimately something about the work of the Holy Spirit.

From Chaos to Promise

Why do we find this mention of the spirit (wind) of God before God spoke his creating words? We have to look at the verb used to describe the spirit's action. Some translations use the word "blowing," others "moving"; but I believe that the best translation is "hovering." The spirit of God was hovering over the waters. The only other place where this verb is used is in Deuteronomy 32:11, where it describes a mother bird beating her wings over her little ones, encouraging them to fly. Unlike the Babylonian myth of creation, in which the chaos is an enemy to be conquered, this formless mess is to be loved and fostered into being. One of the earliest Jewish commentaries on this text, dating from New Testament times, interpreted it this way: "A spirit of *love* before the Lord was blowing (hovering) over the face of the waters."[3] This holy wind is not a part of the chaos, it is God's motherly love conveying the promise of life, order, and beauty to what was of itself a mess. Because God's spirit was hovering over it, chaos became promise.

And so we recognize the relevance of this image for our own lives. At times we feel like our lives are a mess. There is no light, and we are floating about like a cork lost at sea. We try to fight it, to no avail. We try to flee, but there is no exit. What do we do? We fall on our knees and ask the Holy Spirit to hover over our mess, to embrace it lovingly and prepare it for the light of God's word. If you pray in tongues, this is a good way to let your chaotic depths surface and then turn them over to the Lord. As the powerful but wordless Spirit of God prepared for God's cosmic word, the Holy Spirit in our wordless prayer lovingly prepares our chaos for the word that will give shape and meaning to what made no sense before. The Spirit will show us how "God makes all things work together for the good of those who love him" (Romans 8:28).

I have had this experience many times. Once, in emotional pain over something that had happened (I don't remember what), I prayed this way for a good while, letting the depths of my emotions out and giving them to the Holy Spirit. Finally, I opened my Bible, and my eyes fell on Psalm 56:8: "All my tears are held in your flask." I don't remember whether this word changed the outside events, but it brought order out of my chaos—and peace, even joy. That word for me was like God's first word in the darkness, "Let there be light" (Genesis 1:3). The circumstances were no longer oppressing me. I was standing on top of them.

If the Spirit in Genesis 1 is loving encouragement for the hopeless, in the Book of Exodus it is powerful intervention on behalf of God's people. The wind or the breath of God blew open the sea, allowing the Israelites to escape their pursuers, who then perished as God blew the waters back. "At the breath (*ruah*) of your wrath the waters piled up, the flowing waters stood like a mound, the flood waters congealed in the midst of the sea. . . . When your wind (*ruah*) blew, the sea overwhelmed them; like lead they sank in the mighty waters" (Exodus 15:8, 10). St. Augustine applied this imagery to the baptism of new converts: "Your sins were like the Egyptians pursuing you, but only to the Red Sea." Even before the Bishop of Hippo, St. Paul applied the exodus imagery to baptism (1 Corinthians 10:1-4) and hailed the Spirit as freeing us from slavery, whether it be to sin and the flesh (Romans 8:15) or to the old law: "Where the Spirit of the Lord is, there is freedom" (2 Corinthians 3:17).

What joy there was in the hearts of the Israelites as they reached the other side of the sea! What joy I have seen in persons who have been inwardly oppressed but then receive the Spirit of freedom. One day, Ismael, a friend of mine, was driving several of us to a life-chain rally. The topic of beer somehow came up, and he told us this story:

> I had an addiction to beer. I always kept plenty in the refrigerator, and I would drink one beer after another.

This was really messing up my marriage. I made a Life in the Spirit seminar, was prayed over for the baptism in the Spirit, and I have not had a drink since. The Lord even removed my desire for beer. I didn't notice it at first, but after two weeks I happened to see an unopened six-pack in the refrigerator and realized I hadn't touched it. I guess I tempted the Lord on this one, but I went to the supermarket and stood before the shelves loaded with beer. Could I resist grabbing a six-pack? I didn't even feel the urge to. The Holy Spirit had freed me from the spirit of drink.

The Wind of God, the Holy Spirit, had done the exodus once again. Ismael was on the dry land of freedom.

Wind of Rebirth

There is mystery about the wind. There is mystery about the Spirit. "The wind blows where it chooses. You can hear the sound it makes, but you don't know where it comes from or where it goes; so it is with everyone born of the Spirit" (John 3:8). Jesus was explaining to Nicodemus that being born again of water and the Spirit is a mystery that goes beyond the Pharisee's rational categories. This nighttime visitor had thought that his observance of the law and the hundreds of little prescriptions with which the Pharisees had surrounded it was more than enough to put him in right relation with God. And yet, there was something about Jesus, especially his miracles, that made Nicodemus wonder if God might be expecting something else of him. Born again? But that means a complete makeover. We don't know how Nicodemus responded to Jesus' challenge, but Jesus' words must have stayed with him, because he later helped bury Jesus, bringing an enormous mixture of myrrh and aloes (John 19:39-40).

What does it mean for us that the Spirit blows where he chooses? It means that the Holy Spirit is the God of surprises. Just as you can't tell when the wind will fill the sail and carry the boat along, so neither can you predict when and where and how the Spirit will move. This is important. When people are prayed over for the baptism in the Holy Spirit, sometimes the Spirit affects them with tears, sometimes with laughter, sometimes with the gift of tongues, sometimes with resting in the Spirit, and sometimes with no apparent immediate effect. In this last case, the person should not panic or feel disappointed, because sometimes the Holy Spirit comes like a time-release capsule. The receiver may wake up in the middle of the night or the next day with a hunger for Scripture. Or he may notice a gradual change in the way he handles stress or the way he deals with his spouse or his co-workers. But we can rest assured that the Holy Spirit is going to come if he is asked: "If you . . . know how to give good gifts to your children, how much more will the Father in heaven give the Holy Spirit to those who ask him!" (Luke 11:13).

The Wind at Pentecost

Finally, there is the mighty wind that filled the upper room at Pentecost. What did this signal for the disciples and Mary gathered in the upper room—and especially for St. Luke, who was reporting the event? Was it the remembrance of the wind of the Spirit at the first creation or the mighty wind that swept aside the waters of the sea? Both are possible. In either case, the wind was announcing some kind of direct intervention of God. It was certainly an attention getter. (I think of the sudden blast of a Texas "norther" slamming into our house—windows rattling, doors ajar slamming, leaves flying.)

But maybe it recalled another Old Testament story—about Elijah. The pagan queen Jezebel was so angered by Elijah's victory over the four hundred prophets of Baal that she determined to find and kill him within twenty-four hours. Elijah fled to Mount Horeb (Sinai), so exhausted and discouraged after walking a day alone across the desert that he collapsed, asking God to take his life. An angel woke him, refreshed him with bread and water, and told him that he still needed to cross the desert to meet the Lord. Strengthened, he managed to make the forty-day journey. Arriving, he took refuge in a cave. The Lord then overwhelmed him with a series of signs: wind, earthquake, and fire—and then a tiny whispering sound. The first sign was "a strong, powerful wind that split the mountains and shattered rocks" (1 Kings 19:11). The earthquake and the fire must have reminded Elijah of the revelation to Moses on this same spot (Exodus 19:16). But the wind? That was new. And what a wind it was! I have seen gales, and many people have been caught in hurricanes or tornados, but a wind that split mountains and shattered rocks? It was certainly a reminder of the power of God. But God, the text says, was not in the wind; nor was he in the earthquake or in the fire, though all these happened "in front of him." Finally, there was a tiny whispering sound, at which Elijah hid his face and went to the entrance of the cave.

There he heard the Lord's voice giving him a new mission: to anoint a new king for Israel.

Looking back on this scene in the light of Pentecost, what can we learn? We can learn that it is normal for someone in the service of the Lord to experience rejection, even failure at times. We want to give up. But God sends an angel in one form or another to strengthen us, to help us get up and continue the journey. We may still have to cross a desert, but we have the bread of the Eucharist to get us through. We go to a place where we give the Lord a chance to reveal himself to us again. That is our own personal Sinai: a retreat, a Life in the Spirit seminar, or another place of encounter. Sometimes the Holy Spirit comes like a mighty wind. Or an earthquake. Or fire. We might even find ourselves on the floor when we are prayed over. If that is what we need, God will touch us in that way. But the Holy Spirit may touch us in a tiny whisper, if that is what we need. Each of these movements, whether wind or earthquake or fire or whisper, is the Spirit's work, preparing us to hear the word of God. So it was at creation, when the Spirit, hovering over the chaos as wind, readied the formless mass to hear the creating word of God (Genesis 1:1-2). So it was on Mount Sinai, where similar signs preceded God's giving the law to Moses (Exodus 19:16-18). Once we experience this new encounter with the Lord, he sends us on a fresh mission.

Isn't this what happened at Pentecost? The disciples were huddled in the upper room with the doors shut (John would say for fear of the Jews, 20:19). Then came the mighty wind. It crushed the mountains and rocks of their fears, their discouragement, and all those fleshly resources they had depended on. It prepared them to hear the word of God, to proclaim it loudly both within the community and outside it (Acts 2:4; 2:14-41). And that is what happens to us when we receive the Holy Spirit. We may need a rock-crushing wind to break us open. But we may also need that gentle whisper of the Spirit in the silent depths of our heart. Either way, the Holy Spirit brings us new power, new life, and an anointing for mission.

....

Father, your Holy Spirit touches us in so many ways. First you embrace us in our mess, our chaos, just as we are. But that embrace is also promise, as it was at the first creation. When we cannot see because of the darkness, your Spirit prepares us to hear your word: "Let there be light." When we feel lost at sea, your Spirit prepares us to hear your word dividing the waters and letting the dry land appear, as you did at creation, as you did in parting the sea so your people could be free and move to the promised land. Let your mighty wind blow through me, crushing the rocks of my pride and resistance and clearing out everything that is not you. Amen.

Chapter 5

Fire

Winter nights on the ranch in the 1930s would have had all the family shivering if it were not for the fireplace, the only source of heat in the house. The happy magnet that drew us together served another purpose that I appreciated. My mother would put a rock or a brick or a flatiron into the fire until it got warm enough to wrap in a newspaper and a towel and slip it by my feet as I crawled in between the chilled sheets for the night. I learned to love the fire. But there was also an awesome mystery about fire. When we would take a piece of farm equipment to the blacksmith in town, I marveled at what this fire could do to a piece of iron. First the rust peeled off, turning the iron black. Then, slowly the iron turned red, and finally white—so white that it looked as if the iron was part of the fire! And now the blacksmith could shape it as he wished. To my young eyes, this was a miracle made possible by fire.

But I also learned as a boy that fire could destroy. During a particularly severe drought, the ranch workers harvested prickly pears and then used flame throwers to burn off the thorns so that the cattle could eat them. Drought also brought danger of pasture fires, but we were fortunate never to experience any. But the danger was always there. It was only in school that I learned that fire is not only the energy of our sun but also of the billions of suns in the universe. Fire is a power that can be used and cherished, but it must also be respected, because it can destroy you.

At Pentecost the Holy Spirit came as wind but also as fire. In the light of what the disciples and Mary and Luke knew from their biblical tradition, what did this mean? Fire could mean many things. Fire is an attendant of the throne of God (Psalm 50:3; 97:3). God called Moses from a bush that was burning without being consumed (Exodus 3:2). The Lord gave his people a pillar of fire to guide them by night (Exodus 13:21; 14:24; Numbers 14:14). He revealed himself on Sinai, where the whole mountain was enveloped with smoke "because the Lord came down upon it in fire" (Exodus 19:18). The memory of this revelation by fire runs like a thread through the entire Book of Deuteronomy to remind the Israelites of the great wonders the Lord worked for them and also of the peril should they be unfaithful, for the Lord "is a consuming fire" (Deuteronomy 4:24). The Book of Numbers tells us that when the Israelites in the desert built a dwelling for the Lord, the cloud of the exodus rested upon it during the day, and at night it looked like fire. Whenever the cloud moved, whether by day as cloud or at night as fire, the Israelites would follow it; they would never move unless it did (Numbers 9:15-23). Unlike the sacrifice of the prophets of Baal, fire fell from heaven to consume the sacrifice of Elijah (1 Kings 18:23-38), proving that the God of Israel was the true God. Fire often represents the wrath of God against the enemies of Israel (Psalm 89:46; Isaiah 30:27), sometimes as the flaming effect of his breath or spirit (*ruah,* Isaiah 30:33; 33:11). For in Isaiah's mind, the cloud and the fire of Sinai had now moved to Jerusalem (Isaiah 4:5; 31:9; see Psalm 68:18). But this fire can also be directed against God's own people because of their sins and infidelity

(Jeremiah 4:4; 15:14; 17:4). It would be a cleansing judgment by spirit and fire (Isaiah 4:4).

The words of the prophet share in the very fire of God: "'Is not my word like fire?' says the Lord" (Jeremiah 23:29). If Jeremiah tried to hold back the word he had been given, it became a fire within him, and he could not restrain it (20:9). This closeness of fire to the prophetic spirit helps us understand what was happening at Pentecost, because there the tongues of fire were the outward sign of what the Holy Spirit was doing interiorly in each of the disciples. They felt that they *must* let the fire out in praise and bold proclamations.

The Fire of God's Compassion

Even before John the Baptist, the Old Testament prophet said that the Lord one day would come in fire (Isaiah 66:14-15). The Baptist picked this up when he said that the one coming after him would baptize with the Holy Spirit and fire (Matthew 3:11; Luke 3:16). In the light of what John knew of the Old Testament texts (especially Isaiah 4:4, the judgment by spirit and fire) and of the teachings of the Essene monastery at Qumran nearby, which he surely had internalized, it is clear that he was thinking that Jesus would be a fiery judge. And that presented a problem for John when Jesus came to be baptized as a penitent. "I should be baptized by you," he objected (Matthew 3:14); but Jesus insisted, and so John relented. But his misgivings must have persisted, because when the Nazarene began to perform miracles of mercy, John sent his disciples to ask Jesus if he was really the "coming one" or whether they should look for another (Matthew 11:2-6). Nowhere in the Old Testament was anything said about fire being a symbol of mercy. The only association of fire with love was in the Song of Solomon (8:6), but that was talking only about romantic love. Jesus pointed to his miracles of compassion and mercy and then declared blessed anyone who did not take offense at him. John had thought of the fire of God's judgment. Jesus had come with another kind of fire, the fire of God's compassion and mercy.

Jesus also said he had come to cast fire on the earth (Luke 12:49). That meant two things: the fire of his passion and the fire of Pentecost. Concerning the passion, Pope John Paul II wrote,

> The Old Testament on several occasions speaks of "fire from heaven" which burnt the oblations presented by men. By analogy one can say that the Holy Spirit is the "fire from heaven" which works in the depth of the mystery of the Cross. Proceeding from the Father, he directs toward the Father the sacrifice of the Son, bringing it into the divine reality of the Trinitarian communion. If sin caused suffering, now the pain of God in Christ crucified acquires through the Holy Spirit its full human expression.[4]

But the fire that Jesus promised to send was ultimately the Holy Spirit on Pentecost. And the effects of that sending were the same as those of the Spirit upon Jesus—a ministry of healing, transformation, and peace. It would be a different kind of fire. It would purify and transform, yes, but it would be the fire of love and evangelization.

Tongues of Fire

It would come as *tongues* of fire. Luke no doubt chose that form because it led easily to tongues as language. Already Philo, in the first century, recorded a Jewish tradition that when God decided to give his law to humanity, the nations of the world were gathered at Sinai, and the one message of God went out like a fire and transformed itself into all the different languages of the world so that everyone could hear and understand.[5] Although only Israel accepted the law, the other nations were given the chance to do so by this "miracle of tongues of fire." Luke is telling us that Pentecost was another Mount Sinai (remember that Isaiah already said that Sinai had moved to Jerusalem, 31:9; Psalm 68:18). The earlier Sinai prepared and pointed to this Sinai of the final times, the upper room where the fire of God came down and transformed itself into language that all the nations could understand.

We will come back to this scene when we discuss the gift of tongues. Suffice it to say for the time being that not only was Pentecost a new Sinai, it was also the reversal of the curse of the Tower of Babel. In that story, because of human pride in building the tower, the languages of people were confused so that they could no longer communicate with one another. Now the good news could be heard by every nation under heaven. I marveled at this miracle when at an international conference I heard people of many different languages singing in tongues a symphony of praise to God. None was singing in his own language, and yet they were united at a level deeper than any rational language could take them. There was no need for translation, for they found and understood each other in the language of love.

The little community in the upper room was praying as Elijah did on Mount Carmel. And as he did for Elijah (1 Kings 18:24), the Lord answered with fire. And just as the blacksmith's fire transformed iron in front of my young eyes, the Holy Spirit transformed that first community from fearful, confused men and women into a people of praise, proclamation, and witness. The "history of the Spirit" began to unfold in the life of the church. The earliest association of fire with the Holy Spirit appears in Paul's first letter to the Thessalonians, written about A.D. 51. He told his people, "Do not quench the Spirit. Do not despise prophecies" (5:19-20). "Quench" (or "extinguish") is a word used to put out a fire, and here it means the fire of the Holy Spirit that inspires spontaneous, prophetic utterances. The church, Paul wrote, needs the fire of the Holy Spirit; it needs that flame that springs up unbidden to keep the community alive with the word of God.

My grandmother, whose memory went back before electricity and even before matches, told me of one morning when a neighbor boy rode up with a bucket in his hand and said, "Ma'am, can I borrow fire?" The neighbors' fire had died overnight, and he was asking for live coals to get it started again. Sometimes we, too, have to borrow fire. We ask our brothers and sisters to pray over us for the baptism in the Holy Spirit.

The image of fire has helped me in prayer. As I begin to pray, I imagine that my joys, my fears, my worries, the tasks of the day—whatever comes to mind—are logs of wood. As these thoughts and feelings arise, I stack them like logs for a fire. Then

I ask the Holy Spirit to descend as the fire from heaven to consume them, just as the heavenly fire consumed Mount Sinai and the sacrifice of Elijah. What would otherwise be distractions become fuel. As further distractions come, I toss them into the fire. Each one then is no longer a distraction but a holocaust, made so by the Holy Spirit.

....

Lord Jesus, you were faithful to your promise to send the Holy Spirit. You have offered me the same Holy Spirit. Thrust my iron heart into your fire. Burn away its rust, and burn it until I become white hot with your love, until I am one with you. Then melt and mold me into what you want me to be. Open my lips and my tongue to praise you, to proclaim your wonderful works, and to be a witness to you in my world. Mary, you had your Pentecost at the annunciation. You showed the disciples in the upper room how to open themselves to the Holy Spirit. Do the same now for me. Amen.

Chapter 6

Water

Our lawn, once lush with St. Augustine grass, was now four inches of black powder. Sheep were falling into the cracks caused by the drought that had been plaguing Texas for the past seven years, from 1950 to 1957. As a humorous attempt to cope with it, radio stations were playing the sound of rain so that (as they said) children seven and under would not be frightened whenever it did rain. The Medina River, where I swam gleefully as a boy, was a ribbon-sized trickle. My father was shipping his cattle hundreds of miles away where forage could be rented. And eventually he would have to sell off much of the ranch.

The psalmist knew what drought was, and he saw it as an image of the soul longing for God: "My body pines and my soul thirsts for you like earth that is parched, lifeless and without water" (63:1). Obviously the psalmist knew what thirst was. Once, in the Judean desert, I had exhausted my canteen early in the day, and climbing Masada, the desert fortress by the Dead Sea where temperatures reach 120 degrees F in the summer, had left my throat like that parched earth. What a relief it was to get to the oasis Ein Gedi, where water gushed from a cliff into a pool. It reminded me of that desert scene where water flowed from the rock that Moses struck (Numbers 20:2-13).

I went into an emotional and spiritual drought in the summer of 1968. Exhausted, I obeyed the doctor's orders, stopped teaching, and spent six weeks at the ranch. The rest, as well as the experience of my boyhood home, refreshed me physically. But there was still something missing. I didn't realize it at the time, but the Lord was preparing me for the rain of his Holy Spirit, which happened when brothers and sisters in a prayer group prayed over me on Christmas Eve 1970. A new spring-time began, surprising energy flowed into me, and I began to use the Spirit's gifts in my ministry.

Why should I have been surprised? Isaiah promised that when

the spirit from on high will be poured out on us,
    the desert will become an orchard
    and the orchard a forest.
Right will dwell in the desert
    and justice in the orchard.
Justice will bear fruit in peace.
    Right will produce calm and security.
My people will live in peaceful dwellings,
    in safe homes, in secure places of rest . . .
How blessed are you who sow beside every stream
    and let the ox and the donkey range freely!
(Isaiah 32:15-18, 20)

And again:

I will pour out water on the thirsty ground,
    and streams on the dry land;
I will pour out my spirit upon your children,
    my blessing on your descendants.
(Isaiah 44:3)

St. Paul not only saw these prophecies fulfilled in the risen Jesus pouring out the Holy Spirit, he also saw the water from the rock in the desert as the Spirit given by Jesus. The text is a dense one: "Our fathers were all under the cloud, and they all passed through the sea. And they were all baptized into Moses in the cloud and in the sea, and all ate the same spiritual food and drank the same spiritual drink, for they drank from the spiritual rock that followed them, the rock that was Christ" (1 Corinthians 10:1-4). Paul was addressing the Corinthians, who had been selfish, thinking only of themselves and not of their fellow Christians. Some of them had not broken from their pagan habits of sin. He wanted to warn them that just being baptized and receiving the Eucharist and the Holy Spirit was not going to get them into the kingdom if they didn't live up to the holiness of their calling. To convince them, he called on the plight of those who were saved from Egypt in the exodus but whom God found unworthy to admit to the promised land. The cloud represents the Holy Spirit; the sea, the waters of baptism. Moses is a type of Christ. "Baptized into Moses" is a bit awkward, but Paul was thinking of the Christians' baptism into Jesus. The spiritual food, recalling the manna God gave them in the desert, stands for the Eucharist. The spiritual drink could stand for the blood of Christ in the Eucharist, but more likely stands for the Holy Spirit, as does the cloud. For later on in the same letter, Paul wrote, "In one Spirit we were all baptized into one body . . . , and we were all given one Spirit to drink" (1 Corinthians 12:13).

It is not difficult to see the rock in the desert as the type of Christ, from whom the living water of the Spirit flows. But what did he mean by saying that the rock *followed* the Israelites?

Here Paul was doubtless alluding to a tradition of the rabbis who asked how the Israelites could wander around the desert for forty years and draw water from a rock that was stationary. Their solution was simple: God must have arranged for the rock to follow them! The rock joined the pilgrimage! But Paul was thinking of another meaning of "following," the chronological instead of the geographical one. The rock that followed the Israelites in time was Christ, and he provides his people continuously with the water of the Holy Spirit.

A Constantly Flowing Spring

The evangelist John developed this image as "living water." When Jesus, tired from his journey and sitting in the noonday sun, asked the Samaritan woman for a drink, she was surprised that he, a Jew, would even speak to a strange woman, much less a Samaritan, since Jews would not drink from a Samaritan's vessel. Jesus replied, "If you knew who it was that is speaking to you, you might have asked him, and he would have given you living water" (John 4:10). "Living" water normally means spring water, water that is flowing, water in which things can live. She understood it on the natural level and asked where Jesus gets this living water. Jesus explained, "Whoever drinks of this water will thirst again. But whoever drinks of the water I will give will never thirst again, for the water I will give him will become in him a spring of water welling up for eternal life" (John 4:13-14). Here we learn that the Holy Spirit given by Jesus is more than a drink. The Spirit is a constantly flowing spring that will provide refreshment and life into eternity. We are reminded of 1 Thessalonians 4:8, where Paul says that God is giving (constantly) the Holy Spirit to those who receive him.

Here, too, another image from my childhood comes to mind. In the upper pasture, there was a spring we called "Rock Spring," which flowed from the base of a hill. Whenever we rounded up stock near the spring, we would dismount, kneel, and drink from the spring. What pure, sweet water it was and how different from the well water we had back at the ranch and the chlorinated stuff from our taps today! Even now, like David, who yearned for a drink from the well of Bethlehem (2 Samuel 23:15), I think nostalgically of that spring. We didn't realize then that years later people would be bottling and selling such water. But you and I can have much sweeter water if we have the Holy Spirit. He will not merely slake our thirst; he will turn our desert into a garden.

This spring will not just take us to heaven; it *is* heaven. For there, the river of living and life-giving water flows from the throne of God and the Lamb, and wherever the river flows, life flourishes in abundance (Revelation 22:1). The author of the Apocalypse had seen a fulfillment of the vision of Ezekiel, where water flowed from the temple and became a great river full of fish and lined with fruit-bearing trees on its banks (Ezekiel 37:1-12). The temple was gone, replaced by the very persons of God and the Lamb, who pour forth the Holy Spirit, the river of God. That is the dynamic image of the Father, the Son, and the Holy Spirit. And we have the water from that river flowing in us now, thanks to Jesus, giver of the living water.

That is what we learn in another way from John 7:37-39. It was the feast of Tabernacles in Jerusalem, when the largest court of the temple was ablaze at night with four huge candlesticks, and men were dancing, tossing and catching torches. During the day, the priest led a procession to the pool of Siloam and, drawing water in a golden pitcher, processed back to the altar, circled it once, and then poured the water out on the altar as an annual prayer for rain. On the last and greatest day of the feast, he circled the altar seven times before pouring out the water. It was on that day that Jesus stood up and proclaimed, "If anyone thirsts, let him come to me, and let him drink who believes in me. As the Scripture says, from within him will flow rivers of living water." John hastened to add that Jesus said this about the Spirit, whom believers would receive. Does "from within him" refer to the believer or to Jesus? In the light of Jesus' words to the Samaritan woman, we would think that this water would flow from within the believer. On the other hand, moments after Jesus died on the cross, the centurion pierced his side and blood and water flow out. And John, who always had an eye for God's use of symbols, no doubt saw in the blood the Eucharist and in the water the Holy Spirit. Is it possible, then, that John understood Jesus' word "from within him" to mean both from within Jesus and from within the believer? Why not?

What It Takes

But what does it take to receive this living water? When the Samaritan woman asked Jesus for the living water, he replied, "Go, call your husband and come here" (John 4:16). But she didn't have a husband. She had lived with five husbands, and the man she was living with at the time was not her husband. There was sin and disorder in her life. Sin can block the Holy

Spirit. As the Book of Wisdom says, the holy spirit of wisdom does not dwell in a body given to sin and deceit (1:4-5). But sin is no obstacle if the sinner repents according to the sequence Peter gave in Acts 2:38: "*Repent* and be baptized in the name of Jesus Christ that your sins may be forgiven, and you will receive the gift of the Holy Spirit." Repentance begins in the heart with sincere contrition, but confession seals it with the guarantee of God's forgiveness.

The second thing that it takes to receive the living water is simply asking for the release of the Holy Spirit. Jesus, as we have seen already, told us that the Father wants to give us the Holy Spirit more than earthly fathers want to give good gifts to their children (Luke 11:13).

The third thing is not so obvious. Remember that the Holy Spirit is living water. In the Holy Land, there are two bodies of water. Both are fed by the fresh waters of the Jordan River. The larger sea is fifty miles long and thirteen hundred feet deep. But nothing can live in its waters, and thus it is called the Dead Sea. The other sea is much smaller, no more than fifteen miles long and seven miles wide. It is not half as deep. Yet it is today, just as it was in Jesus' time, the center of a major fishing industry. (I know there are fish, because when I went swimming there and stood on the sandy bottom, the fish came up and nibbled at my toes. Or maybe they were welcoming me by kissing my feet—nobody else had ever done that!) What is the difference between these two seas? Why is one of them living water, the other the Dead Sea? The difference is that the Sea of Galilee passes on the water it receives, while the Dead Sea does not. Its water just evaporates.

If the Holy Spirit is living water, then for the water to continue to be alive, to refresh us, it must somehow get out. How does that happen? We call the outlets the charisms of the Spirit. The sacraments get the Holy Spirit in. The charisms get the Holy Spirit out. In practical terms, what that means is that there must be some outward expression of the gift of the Spirit if the gift is to be kept alive. What are those outward expressions? We will treat them in detail later, but for now let's look at how the Holy Spirit got "out" in the early disciples. At Pentecost the disciples burst into praise. It took the form not only of tongues but also shouts of acclamation and proclamation. So the first outward expression of the Spirit is spontaneous praise. The gift of tongues, as we shall explain in detail later, wells up from the heart and bypasses known words, simply because God "is too much for words."

But there are other forms of praise, too. And if there is a gift of tongues, there is also a gift of ears, spiritual ears to hear the word of God in a new, living way and then to speak what you hear. Another outlet is the gift of healing. I remember praying over Monique, a teenager who said she was "dying" to receive the Holy Spirit, and when I prayed over her, her hands turned very warm and she began immediately praying for people. The people for whom she prayed "rested" in the spirit. Resting in the Spirit is that sense of being so overcome by the love of God, the Holy Spirit, that one just needs to lie or sit while the Lord heals at a deep level. I like to call resting in the Spirit God's anesthesia so he can perform gentle spiritual surgery.

A less noticeable but nonetheless important expression of the life in the Spirit is gifts of service, which could take many forms. If you were prayed over for the baptism in the Spirit and felt moved to help set up or take down the chairs, and you had never done that before, that could be the first indication of a gift of the Spirit. But if you feel led to serve, don't neglect the gift of praise, because it will keep you refreshed even as you serve. As soon as Mary received the Holy Spirit at the annunciation, she hastened to be of service to her cousin Elizabeth, but she also burst out in her song of praise that we call the Magnificat.

....

Lord Jesus, you promised living water to those who ask it in faith. Flood my desert with the water of your Holy Spirit. Slake my thirst with the sweet spring water of your Spirit. Holy Spirit, show me how you want to move through me in praise, proclamation, healing, and service. Amen.

Chapter 7

Dove

D o you remember the photo of white doves hovering around Pope John Paul II as he stood at his window during one of his last public appearances? A coincidence? I have that picture on my desk. I also remember attending a public audience with Pope Benedict XVI when white doves circled over the piazza. And, strange enough, shortly before the pope's appearance, two clouds could be seen above St. Peter's, and if I had to tell you what they looked like, my best answer would be angel wings. Coincidences? Of course. But could God use coincidences as signs? Of course. If you believe in a loving God who wants a personal relationship with you, you can see his signs everywhere, in the wonders of nature and, yes, in coincidences.

Coincidence or not, the dove that descended on Jesus at his baptism (in bodily form, Luke insists, 3:22) was a sign clearly intended by God to manifest the Holy Spirit's coming upon Jesus. Of course, this was not the first time Jesus was united with the Holy Spirit, because that had happened at his very conception. That was in the hidden silence of Mary's womb, and even Mary knew only by faith that it had happened. In Jesus' baptism, there was an outward confirmation that he was the one anointed by the Holy Spirit to announce and introduce the kingdom of God. This was his anointing for mission. Mark didn't mention that the phenomenon was seen by anyone else, but focused rather on Jesus' personal experience of the event (1:9-11). Luke did the same (3:22), as the voice from heaven said, "*You* are my beloved son. . . ." But Matthew (3:17) said it slightly differently: "*This* is my beloved son, . . ." to suggest more explicitly that the Father is pointing out the revelation to us, the readers. Using the same words at the transfiguration, the Father would add, "Listen to him!" (Matthew 17:5).

Three Manifestations of God

The alighting of the dove upon Jesus is the central one of three important manifestations of God. The first manifestation is when the heavens are torn open. Mark used the very graphic word *torn* in his description of Jesus' baptism, suggesting a sudden if not violent rending of the heavens. He used the same verb when at the moment of Jesus' death the curtain of the temple was "torn" in two (15:38). The tearing open of the heavens forecasted the victory Jesus would win by his death. The two tearings are like bookends, giving keys to the mission of Jesus. The heavens were slammed shut by Adam's sin, and the prophet longed for them to be opened again: "Oh, that you would tear open the heavens and come down!" (Isaiah 63:19). Prior to the death of Jesus, God's presence in the holy of holies was hidden behind a curtain through which no one could pass except the high priest once a year on the Day of Atonement. But with Jesus' death on the cross, all barriers to heaven were stripped away and immediate access to God is available to all.

The second manifestation of God is the descent of the dove, clearly identified in all four gospels as the sign of the Holy Spirit. Why the dove? In many cultures the dove is a sign of peace but also a sign of love. My older brothers had formed a teenage band of guitar, mandolin, and violin, and their Mexican music teacher introduced them to mariachi music. Until they all had to leave for World War II, our home was filled with mariachi music. And a dove "flew" through many a song they played. Some songs even had the word "dove" in their titles, such as "La Paloma" and "Cucurrucu, Paloma." In Mexican music, the dove is the favorite symbol of love.

So it is also in the great love song of Solomon, where the gentle bird appears six times as a sign of romantic, marital love (1:15; 2:14; 4:1; 5:2, 12; 6:9). Love appears in the baptism of Jesus, but it is the love of God the Father for his Son, whom he calls his beloved (Matthew 3:17; Mark 1:11; Luke 3:22). Those familiar with the Bible will remember another beloved son, Abraham's "only son, the beloved" (Genesis 22:2), whom God told Abraham to offer back to him in sacrifice. It was only a test, of course, because there was a lamb to be offered instead, the Lamb of God, who would offer himself in place of all the Isaacs of the world, you and me. God blessed Abraham because "you did not withhold from me your own beloved son" (22:12). How beautiful, God must have thought, was Abraham's love for his son. But how beautiful that Abraham would be willing to let his son, the only promise of the patriarch's posterity, go back into the hands of the Giver. Did the Father see in Abraham's sacrificial love an image of his own that would give up his divine Son, the Lamb sacrificed on the altar of the cross by the hands of sinners, that those very sinners might be saved? As Abraham received his son back alive (Hebrews 11:19), so would the Father, who would not leave his Son in the tomb but would bring him back alive and glorious. It was the Father's love that gave up his only Son to death (John 3:16), and the Father's love that raised him from the dead. *And that love was the Holy Spirit* (Romans 1:1-4).

That love was also a love for us; in fact, it was because of his love for us that he did it. That appeared already at the baptism of Jesus, for there Jesus was anointed for his mission. As the Holy Spirit hovered over the waters of the Jordan in the form of a dove, we are reminded of the creation story in Genesis when the Spirit of God hovered over the waters and readied them to hear the creative word of God. Something cosmic was happening when Jesus was baptized. With Jesus, God was sending his Spirit to renew the face of the earth.

Watching the waters of the great flood finally beginning to recede, Noah sent out a dove to see if any dry land had appeared. It returned with an olive leaf, indicating that out of the vast watery expanse a new creation was beginning (Genesis 8:11). A new creation was also beginning with the baptism of Jesus. When Jesus was baptized, God was starting to make the world anew. The Dove (the Holy Spirit) tells us so.

The third manifestation of God is the voice of the Father: "You are my beloved Son; in you I am well pleased" (Luke 3:22). The Father not only identified Jesus as his Son but told us of his delight in him. If you are a parent, think of the joy you felt when you held your first child for the first time. Theologian and author Scott Hahn told me that this experience for him was the beginning of his conversion to the Catholic Church. If he felt so much love for his child, what must be the Father's love for Jesus! Also, what must be the Father's love for Scott! If the grace of Jesus' baptism is conferred on us when we are baptized, it means that the same three wonders happen: heaven is opened for us, and we can climb like children into the Father's arms; the Holy Spirit comes upon us; and God tells us we are his beloved sons and daughters. More than that, if the baptism of Jesus was his anointing for mission, so is ours. Every time a baby or an adult is baptized, God is starting over to make the world anew! Each of us has a mission, and it is important to discover what it is.

Launching Us on Our Mission

I was baptized as an infant, so I certainly didn't realize the Gift that I had received. The Dove had settled invisibly in my soul but tiny enough not to exceed the dimensions of my mind and heart. The Dove grew within me as I grew, as I learned to pray, and as I received my confirmation at the age of twelve. The most important thing I remember about my confirmation was the pledge that the archbishop made us take that we would not touch hard liquor until the age of twenty-one. Not bad, because the Lord had another kind of intoxication in mind for me. But that was a long way off. He called me to the religious life and later to the priesthood, and these were certainly visitations of the Holy Spirit. But when I was prayed over for the release of the Holy Spirit on Christmas Eve 1970, it was as if the Dove now was ready to fly, and fly she did, taking me with her!

I felt the heavens torn open, giving me a new intimacy with the Father, who said to me in a new, experiential way, "You are my beloved son." These were no longer words. They were an experience, a discovery of *Abba*. Many people say that the baptism in the Spirit gives them a new, living relationship with

Jesus. For me it was primarily an experience of God as my loving Father. Perhaps this was because my relationship with my earthly father had been far from perfect, and this had affected my image of God. My father was a big man, six feet tall and 280 pounds, and when he wore his boots and Stetson, he looked to me like God. He was not only boss of the house, he was also its patriarch. And he had a temper. He had shown me love, but mostly by doing things for me. I never felt emotionally close to him. And this inevitably affected my relationship with God. But the Dove began a process of healing in me, until now I can't wait to see my father in heaven, in the company of him after whom all fatherhood is named (Ephesians 3:14-15).

But the Dove also launched me on a new mission in my life—under obedience, of course, but with a new vitality and new opportunities. I began to seek and use the gifts of the Holy Spirit. I began to write about the Holy Spirit. I was invited to speak at conferences internationally. None of this had been in my plans or dreams. There was also a lot of work to be done on me interiorly, and there still is, but the Holy Spirit doesn't seem to mind.

....

Father, please send your Dove upon me as you did upon Jesus, as you did in my baptism and at other times in my life when I didn't even realize it. But this time let me know it in a new way. Let me know that I am the work of your love, that you love me here and now. And then empower me, as you did Jesus, to go about doing the kind of work he did, bringing light and healing and love to others, so that they, too, may know you and Jesus Christ whom you have sent (John 17:3). Amen.

Chapter 8

Cloud

Summer was my favorite time on the ranch. It often meant work, but even that I loved, because I could show my older brothers and the ranch hands that I could do a man's work—or almost. One of my favorite pastimes was watching those beautiful cumulus clouds that plied the sky like an armada of silent ships, with their gray flat-bottomed keels and cotton-puff sails against the deep blue heavenly sea. Beautiful, indeed, but also mysterious. How were they born from the low-lying morning Gulf clouds? Why were their shapes constantly changing? Why were they all at the same altitude? Why did they vanish when the sun set, and where did they go? I had no control of them. They came and went as they pleased. That's why I loved the song I later learned that began, "Rows and floes of angel hair and ice cream castles in the air, and feather canyons everywhere . . ." The song ended with the line, "I really don't know clouds at all."[6] Indeed, there is hardly a better symbol of mystery, and it is cross-cultural. In Chinese art, the cloud frequently appears as part of a painting, indicating the contrast between the visible world and the invisible, between the known and the unknown, between material and mystery.

I think God must have been impressed with the clouds he made, because he chose them, the Bible says, to ride on (Psalm 104:3). More important, he chose a cloud as a manifestation of his presence to his people. He manifested his glory in a cloud

(Exodus 16:10). He led his people with a cloud by day (13:21-22; 14:19). And he came down in a cloud that covered Mount Sinai at the time of sealing the covenant with his people (19:16; 24:15, 18). When Moses built the tabernacle, the cloud came down and overshadowed it, and "the glory of the Lord filled the dwelling" (40:34-35). When Solomon dedicated the temple, the cloud of glory filled the holy place (1 Kings 8:10-11).

In the New Testament, a cloud overshadowed Jesus at the transfiguration (Matthew 17:5: Mark 9:7; Luke 9:34). Up to this point, none of these passages made any reference to the Holy Spirit. However, Paul used the cloud of the exodus as an explicit image of the Holy Spirit when he said that "our fathers . . . were all baptized in the cloud and in the sea" (1 Corinthians 10:1-2). For Paul, the sea was the waters of baptism, and the cloud was the Holy Spirit in whom all Christians are baptized (1 Corinthians 12:13). So we are certainly justified in seeing the cloud of the Old Testament, witness of the power and the presence of God, as a "type" of the Holy Spirit.

Overshadowed by the Holy Spirit

That helps us understand better the angel's reply to Mary when she asked how she was to be a mother when she was a virgin. "The Holy Spirit will come upon you," he explained, "and the power of the Most High will *overshadow* you. That is why the Holy One to be born of you will be called Son of God" (Luke 1:35). "The power of the Most High" is parallel to "the Holy Spirit" and is its equivalent. The word "overshadow" is the same word used in the Greek Old Testament, known to Luke for the holy cloud "overshadowing" the tabernacle, the temple, and the transfiguration of Jesus. Mary became the tabernacle of the Son of God by the overshadowing of the Holy Spirit. The Holy Spirit, Mary, and Jesus are intimately united in a common mystery. The same evangelist, Luke, told us that Mary was with the disciples in the upper room at Pentecost (Acts 1:14). But in a real sense she received her personal Pentecost when the Holy Spirit overshadowed her and worked the miracle of the incarnation of the Son of God in her womb. Luke also showed her as the perfect cooperator with the plan of God and the movement of the Holy Spirit, for she said, "Be it done to me according to your word" (Luke 1:38), and her faith was praised not only by Elizabeth (1:45) but by Jesus, as well (11:28).

So what does the image of the cloud tell us about the Holy Spirit, and what do these scriptural passages tell us about receiving the Holy Spirit?

First of all, the cloud suggests that the Holy Spirit is mystery. Like the wind, the cloud comes and goes as it will, and "so it is with everyone who is born of the Spirit" (John 3:8). The Holy Spirit is the God of surprises. We cannot program clouds, and we cannot program the Spirit. Every visitation is a gift. But clouds move on, as the cloud in the desert did, and if we experience the Spirit's momentary departure, it may be that he is calling us to move out of our settled comfort to the next stage of our journey. The Israelites, however, did not move unless the cloud moved. Scripture makes that very clear: "If the cloud did not lift, they would not set out until it lifted" (Exodus 40:37). So sometimes the Holy Spirit wants us to stay put and wait. That is not easy for eager, impatient travelers. I know I have at times run ahead of the Cloud. And each time, I have learned my lesson. We need the Spirit's gift of discernment to know when to move and when to sit still.

Clouds cannot be captured. We can't throw a net around them or bottle them or freeze them for further use. We cannot do that with friendships, nor can we do so with the Holy Spirit. We can, however, avoid those things that would "sadden the Holy Spirit" (Ephesians 4:30)—and that means sin of any kind.

Sometimes we not only see the cloud, but we are in it. This happened to Peter, James, and John at the transfiguration of Jesus (Luke 9:34). They were frightened by the experience. This can happen to us also, because we are in the totally unfamiliar territory of the divine, which is beyond our comprehension. The saints and mystics have spoken of this "cloud of unknowing." But it is precisely in the cloud that we can, like the disciples, hear the voice of the Father saying, "This is my Son, my chosen one. Listen to him" (Luke 9:35). And there, too, Jesus can speak to us as he did to his disciples when they were frightened by their experience of the divine, "Courage, it is I; be not afraid" (Matthew 14:27). The Holy Spirit can lead us beyond our comfort zone to meet Jesus and the Father in a deeper, purer way, even if the newness at first is frightening and confusing.

Finally, we can learn from the mother of Jesus how to live with the Cloud, the Holy Spirit. The Spirit overshadowed her as the new and perfect tabernacle, the dwelling place of God. It was her baptism in the Holy Spirit. We enter the Cloud when we are baptized (1 Corinthians 10:1-2). Like Mary, our hearts should always be in the Cloud. But, like Mary, our feet should be on the ground, as were hers on the road to Elizabeth.

....

Holy Spirit, I know that you overshadowed me when I was baptized. But now, come and renew that gift. May your holy Cloud overshadow me. But do more. Take me into the Cloud, take me into yourself, and fill me with your love so that I may know and love the Father and the Son as you do. Mary, spouse of the Holy Spirit, show me how to say yes to the espousal of my spirit with the Holy Spirit. And while my head and my heart should always be in the Cloud, may my feet be ready to take me to those in need. Amen.

Chapter 9

Anointing

"The Spirit of the Lord is upon me, because he has anointed me" (Luke 4:18). These words of Jesus rang like a trumpet blast in the synagogue at Nazareth to proclaim the inauguration of his public mission. Since he connected the Holy Spirit with an anointing, and since the very name "Christ" means "Anointed One," let us explore this rich concept, hoping to discover why God chose "anointing" to tell us who Jesus is and what role the Holy Spirit has in Jesus' mission.

In the Old Testament, kings and priests were anointed. Thus, Samuel anointed Saul (1 Samuel 10:1) and David (16:13), the earliest in a long line of anointed kings. After their anointing, the Spirit rushed on Saul and David (10:10; 16:13). Priests, too, were anointed so that each of them, like the kings, could be called an anointed one (Exodus 40:13-15). The finest of oil was used for this purpose.

Why oil? Along with wheat and wine, oil was considered one of the greatest blessings of daily life. It was used for cooking, for fueling lamps, for providing cooling refreshment when poured on the head, and for healing. It was associated with rejoicing, as references to the "oil of gladness" indicate (Psalm 45:7; Isaiah 61:3). The psalmist praised oil because it made the face shine (Psalm 104:15). It is not surprising, then, that it was used widely in the religious life of Israel. It fueled the lamps for the dwelling of the Lord (Exodus 25:6) and was used for the consecration of objects (Genesis 28:18), especially the dwelling and its altar (Exodus 40:9-11). It was used to bake the cakes and wafers used in the ordination of priests (29:2). And it was mixed with the cereal offerings (Leviticus 2:1). And as mentioned above, anointing with oil was a key element in the installation of kings and the ordination of priests.

The Holy Spirit Is the Oil

But there was one group of influential persons in the Old Testament that was not anointed with oil: the prophets. Their anointing came directly from God and did not require a rite of installation with oil. Moses was called directly by God, and it was he who anointed Aaron, just as the prophet Samuel anointed Saul and David but was not himself anointed. This was significant because in ancient Israel, kingship and priesthood were understood to be dependent on prophecy or on the spirit of God, if you will.

Thus, Jesus himself, though priest and king, was not anointed with oil. He was anointed directly by the Holy Spirit of God (Acts 10:38), as Jesus proclaimed, "The Holy Spirit is upon me, because he has anointed me" (Luke 4:18). Why did Jesus use the word "anoint," which suggests oil or ointment, if there was no material oil by which he was anointed? Because the Holy Spirit was the oil! What oil did for the priests and kings of the Old Testament the Holy Spirit did for Jesus, and this, not just because he was a prophet and as such did not need to be anointed, but because Jesus' anointing constituted him as the Son of God. That is what happened at the moment that Jesus took flesh in the womb of Mary. His very conception was the work of the Holy Spirit, and that is why he is called "the Son of God" (Luke 1:35).

Jesus shares that anointing with us through our baptism. In a dense passage, Paul says, "The one who confirms us with you in our union with Christ and has anointed us is God himself, who sealed us and gave us the Spirit in our hearts as the first installment" (2 Corinthians 1:21-22). There is a beautiful alliteration in the Greek: *Christon kai chrisas*, which we can only approximate in English by translating as, "God confirms us in union with his *Anointed One*, and he *anointed* us too." Was oil used in the earliest baptisms? We can't be sure; we do know that the gesture for the conveying of the Holy Spirit was the laying on of hands, and there is no mention of oil as part of the rite in the New Testament. The Holy Spirit *is* the anointing. But we also know that shortly after, oil was used in the baptismal rite, as it continues to be used today in both baptism and confirmation. It signifies the Holy Spirit.

And it also signifies consecration. Just as altars and vessels by their anointing were reserved exclusively for God and his service, so the anointing by the Holy Spirit, whether externally ritualized by oil or not, consecrates the person as belonging totally to God in Christ, the Anointed One.

That means that we are different because we are anointed. "Do you not know that your body is a temple of the Holy Spirit, who is within you, whom you have from God, and that you are not your own? You have been bought at a price. So glorify God in your body" (1 Corinthians 6:19-20).

From that dignity flow many consequences. If the Holy Spirit anoints, then a number of the traits of anointing oil can be attributed to him. Among these is healing. When the Good Samaritan tended the wounds of the man who had been beaten by robbers, he poured wine and oil on them—wine to disinfect, oil to soothe. Following the lead of the sermons by Fathers of the church, we can say that the Good Samaritan is Jesus, who came to brutalized humanity to apply the wine of his saving blood and the oil of the Holy Spirit. When Jesus sent out his disciples to heal, they anointed the sick with oil (Mark 6:13). Jesus himself did not do so, but the disciples' use of oil signified that the healing power came not from themselves but from the Anointed One.

Anointing also expresses a bond of love between the anointer and the anointed. That's what happened when the woman anointed Jesus' feet (Luke 7:46-47; John 12:3). When we are anointed with the Holy Spirit, the anointing Father and the anointing Son express their love for us (Romans 5:5).

As anointing oil was called the oil of gladness, so joy is one of the chief fruits of the Holy Spirit, the first mentioned after love (Galatians 5:22).

And since the anointing consecrates us, we are holy and are challenged to live out that holiness in our daily lives. We no longer belong to ourselves but to Christ, the Anointed One. By our baptism, we are made priests, prophets, and kings with Jesus. And like him, we are given a mission: as priests, to offer our world to the Father; as prophets, to witness to the gospel in the territory assigned to us by God's providence; and as kings, to extend God's kingdom to the world.

Finally, another effect of this anointing is a clear knowledge of the truth about Jesus. The community to which John was writing his first letter was being badgered by false teachers and reduced in numbers by the defection of some of its members. To those who had remained faithful, John wrote, "You have an anointing from the Holy One, and you all have knowledge. . . . The anointing you have received from him remains in you, and you have no need for anyone to teach you, but as his anointing teaches you about everything and is true and not false, and just as it taught you, remain in him" (1 John 2:20, 27). The "Holy One" is probably Jesus, the risen Lord, and the anointing is the Holy Spirit. What is remarkable is that, while John did clarify the proper teaching about Jesus, he expected the persevering fidelity of his readers and their understanding of the truth to come not from a command of his but from the interior teaching of the Holy Spirit. The Holy Spirit provides a litmus test for orthodoxy. If the Holy Spirit is spiritual oil in the soul, it will not allow the water of heresy to be mixed with it.

....

Heavenly Father, I am awed by the multitude of ways you show your love for us. Deepen in me the awareness that I have been anointed and consecrated by your Holy Spirit for a noble mission. Mary, you in whom the first anointing of Jesus took place, show me how to live with the Holy Spirit in me as he was in your heart. Amen.

Chapter 10

Paraclete

Vested in his black robe, the district judge took his seat at the bench and pored over the motion submitted by the female lawyer, who was also dressed in black. To her right stood the accused, a twenty-one-year-old man, whom I here call David, dressed in a grey suit. And to David's right stood another person dressed in black—me—in my clergy suit and Roman collar.

It had been three years since David's wild senior year in high school, when he had used and even sold drugs and had totaled the family car. Since then, he had experienced a conversion. He was now praying daily and had found a mentor in me.

David thought his past was behind him, until—three years later—the sheriff knocked at the family door with a warrant for his arrest. A man caught selling drugs had made a plea bargain and received a lighter sentence by turning David in for selling drugs to him three years earlier. Standing next to David, I said nothing, nor was I asked to speak; but, attached to the lawyer's motion was a letter I had written on David's behalf. It said that David had become a wonderful person and was now zealously helping others get off drugs. I was afraid that if David went to jail, his spiritual formation would be thwarted, and he might even be sucked into the ways of fellow felons. That's why I stood at his side as he faced the judge, and that's why I wrote the letter. David got probation and continued to grow in the Lord.

I was a paraclete.

In biblical times, a paraclete was a supportive witness. Translations of the Greek word differ: "advocate," "comforter," "helper," or simply "paraclete." The word literally means "called to one's side." It has sometimes been suggested that the paraclete is a lawyer who pleads one's case, but in biblical times there is no evidence that there were people who acted in such a capacity. Instead, accuser and accused appeared before a judge with their respective witnesses, and the judge made his decision after listening to their testimonies. The outcome of the case depended largely on the successful testimony of the witnesses, the paracletes.

A Human Image of the Holy Spirit

And so we come for the first time to a human image of the Holy Spirit, the Paraclete. Unlike the other images, which are from the material or the animal world (the dove), "paraclete" implies personhood. This is confirmed by the fact that Jesus called the Holy Spirit *another* Paraclete, a person like himself, though not visibly incarnate as Jesus is. This is a huge step forward, and it allows us (from a canonical point of view, the scholars would say) to read other New Testament references to the Holy Spirit as personal, even though *pneuma* ("spirit") is neuter in Greek and could be grammatically referred to as "it." Thus, when Paul said that "the love of God has been poured into our hearts through the Holy Spirit *that* has been given to us" (Romans 5:5, New American Bible translation), we are fully justified in translating his words as, "*who* has been given to us." (Revised Standard Version, Catholic Edition).

We owe the paraclete image to the Gospel of John. There the Holy Spirit bore witness to Jesus after his resurrection in the person of his disciples against the accusations of the world (16:8-10), whether "world" meant the Jewish authorities who crucified Jesus, the Pharisaic leaders who were fighting the early church's claim that Jesus was the Messiah, or the pagan world that saw Christianity as a threat to its gods and its worldly culture. The Holy Spirit stood beside the church and showed the world's claims to be false. When the Paraclete comes, Jesus said, "he will convict the world about sin, and justice, and condemnation" (John 16:8). He will show up disbelief for what it is. He will show that God's justice reversed the verdict of the Jewish court by raising Jesus from the dead and returning him to the Father. And although the Jewish authorities had condemned Jesus, his death was really the condemnation of Satan, "the ruler of this world." The meaning, then, of "paraclete" is primarily "witness," as Jesus himself said: "When the Paraclete comes . . . he will testify on my behalf" (15:26).

The witnessing Spirit appears again in 1 John 5:6-10, a dense passage that will reward our careful examination:

This is the one who came in water and blood, Jesus Christ, not in the water only but in the water and the blood. And the Spirit is the one who testifies, for the Spirit is the truth. Thus there are three who testify: the Spirit and the water and the blood, and these three agree. If we accept the witness of men, the witness of God is greater, for that is the witness God gave about his Son. He who believes in the Son of God has that witness in himself.

Scholars have debated at great length the different elements of this text. One explanation is that John was countering a heresy that maintained that the divinity of Christ came upon Jesus at his baptism but left him on the cross. Another explanation is that water refers to baptism and blood to the Eucharist. Finally, other authors focus on the death of Jesus on the cross, where water and blood gushed from his side at the thrust of the centurion's spear. That leads nicely into the role of the Spirit, for John describes the moment of Jesus' death not as simply breathing his last (as Matthew and Mark do) or of handing over his spirit to the Father (as Luke did), but rather, "he handed over *the Spirit,*" playing on the double meaning of Jesus' breathing his last and handing over the Spirit as his ultimate gift.

These three elements, then, the Spirit, the water, and the blood, would bear witness to Jesus. How so? John does not say, but we can assume that at the very least each of these elements fulfills promises made in the Scriptures. The Spirit, manifested in the last breath of Jesus, is the Spirit foretold by the prophets. The water fulfills the promise of living water "flowing from within him" (John 7:38). And the blood bears witness by showing that Jesus is the sacrificial Lamb of God (Isaiah 53:7).

But where is that witness to be found? In the heart of the one who believes: "He who believes . . . has that witness within himself" (1 John 7:10). This correlates well with the role of the Holy Spirit in the Gospel of John about the witnessing Spirit. It is first of all within the believer that the Spirit testifies. The Holy Spirit, experienced in the believer's heart, is sufficient proof of the truth of Jesus.

But out of that interior witness, the Holy Spirit also gives the power to witness in and to the world. The accusers today may not be quite the same as those the earliest disciples had to face, but the adversaries are many. In some countries, Christians are being persecuted and killed. In other countries, the media are biased against the church. Family values are being assaulted. Christians in the Roman Empire were tempted by the sensuous theaters, but those theaters were not in their living rooms or on the Internet. Today we cannot avoid all exposure to evil, but the Holy Spirit within us provides a gyroscope or homing device that tells us where the true route lies and helps us keep a stable course toward the goal. When we are guided by the Spirit, we have a spiritual sense of smell that detects instantly the fetid odor of evil. At the same time, the disciples, through whom the Spirit continues to witness, will do greater works even than Jesus did (John 14:12) so that the world may believe.

The Spirit of Truth

Jesus calls the Paraclete the Spirit of truth. The only place the expression "the Spirit of truth" occurs before the New Testament is in the Dead Sea scrolls. There it means the angel, probably Michael, who will lead the "sons of light" in the final battle with the powers of darkness. He is a militant angel, very much like the angel Michael who appears in the Apocalypse as the heavenly defender of the church. That idea of militancy seems to be behind the description of the Paraclete as the Spirit of Truth, though certainly he is more than an angel. So "truth" here means more than doctrinal truth. It has the sense of loyal commitment and readiness to engage the enemies of the church, much as we speak of a "true friend" as one we can count on in time of trouble. It was the same Holy Spirit that enabled Jesus to cast out the evil spirits: "If it is by the Spirit of God that I cast out demons, then the kingdom of God has come upon you" (Matthew 12:28). Satan is powerless against the Holy Spirit.

Judith MacNutt, well known for her healing ministry, tells of the time a man came to her office, sat down in the chair used for her clients, and introduced himself like this: "I am a high priest of Satan, and I've come here to destroy your work." Judith looked up at the crucifix and replied, "My boss defeated your boss a long time ago." With that, the man stared, jumped up, and ran out of the office screaming.

Sr. Margaret Carew, a lifelong friend of mine with a disarming Irish wit, served in the Bexar County jail for thirty years, ministering to convicts so that she could pray with them for the baptism in the Holy Spirit. One day an inmate came to her office, sat down, and said, "I've got a razor blade in my pocket, and I am going to cut your throat!"

Sr. Margaret reached out, took his hands in hers, looked him straight in the eye, and with a twinkle in her own said, "Well, I'm glad you are interested in me!"

This melted him, and he said, "I don't believe in God. He never answers my prayers!"

"Do you have a child?" Sr. Margaret asked.

"Yes, a three-year-old boy," he replied.

"Would you give him that razor blade?"

"No way," he said.

"Well, God is a loving Father, and maybe you're asking for the wrong thing."

Later, the inmate came to Sr. Margaret and said, "I prayed that I might escape back to the street, and I got there. I was running from the cops, dashing between cars, and I got hit by three of them. I guess God wanted to teach me a lesson. He gave me what I wanted. But from now on, maybe I should ask for the right things." Eventually, Sr. Margaret was able to pray with him for the baptism in the Holy Spirit.

I tell these stories because in both cases the Paraclete stood by Judith and Sr. Margaret and gave them the words to say on the spur of the moment, as Jesus had promised: "Don't worry about how you should speak or what you should say. You will be given at that moment what you are to say. For it will not be you who are speaking, but the Spirit of your Father speaking through you" (Matthew 10:19-20).

So if, through our faith, we find ourselves in a tight spot, we can count on the Holy Spirit to be there. But not only in tight spots. I have heard children say really inspired things. Audrey told me of her three-year-old nephew Paul, who was sitting on her knee. She risked asking him, "Paul, did you ever think of giving your life to Jesus?"

"How do I do that?" he asked.

Audrey very wisely said, "Well, maybe if you ask him, he'll tell you."

Paul's little brow knit as he thought for a long while. Finally, he formed his hands as if he were holding a ball, then tossed it, and said aloud to Jesus, "Catch!"

Out of the mouths of children.

Ruth, a friend of mine, was reading a book I had written on Mary, entitled *The Woman and the Way: A Marian Path to Jesus.* It basically is a program for spiritual growth under the guidance of the Blessed Virgin. Ruth's four-year-old daughter, Laura, felt she wasn't getting enough of her mother's attention.

"Mom," she asked, "What are you reading?"

"It's a book about Mary," she replied

"Oh Mom, you don't have to read that book. All it says is 'Listen to your Mother!'"

Where do those occasional nuggets of wisdom come from? Are children in their innocence closer to the baptismal grace of the Holy Spirit?

And speaking of children, another text comes to mind. When Jesus was at the Last Supper and was about to leave his disciples, he said, "I will not leave you orphaned. I will come back to you" (John 14:18). How will Jesus come back? The most obvious answer is through his resurrection. But Jesus had just been speaking of the Paraclete, and we know that Jesus in his resurrected body would, even after the resurrection, return to the Father. So the better understanding is that he will return in a permanent way through his Holy Spirit, of whom he had just said, "He will be with you always; . . . he remains with you and will be in you" (John 14:16-17). An orphan is a child without a parent. No matter who else may take over the parent's role, the one left without a real parent is an orphan. Not so the disciples, Jesus said. Why? Because the Holy Spirit will be with them. Was Jesus indicating that the Holy Spirit would mother us in his absence? Among the many attributes of the Spirit, maternal ones are not lacking. And would Mary, proclaimed mother of the disciples from the cross, be the permanent, visible sign of that motherly care? It is tempting to think so. Pope John Paul II spoke of "her motherhood in the Holy Spirit."[7]

Jesus also said that "the Paraclete, the Holy Spirit, will teach you everything and remind you of all that I have told you" (John 14:26). The Holy Spirit would teach the church in the absence of Jesus, and that is why the church would be free from error. John even said that if the anointing (the Holy Spirit) received by the disciples remained in them, they would not need anyone to teach them, because "his anointing teaches you about everything and is true and not false" (1 John 2:27). Of course, John is not denying the need for authoritative teachers in the church; otherwise he would not have written this letter, which is a teaching.

I have been teaching about the Lord all my adult life, and I know that if the Holy Spirit does not teach interiorly, my teaching is just words in the wind. The same is true of preaching. Many times when I am preaching to a Spirit-filled congregation, I feel that the Holy Spirit in the listeners is telling me what to say. Many, too, are the testimonies of those who, once they receive the Holy Spirit, have an insatiable thirst for the word of God. Suddenly, the Scriptures, formerly obscure, become alive and personal, like a letter from a loved one.

The Holy Spirit does not impart a new revelation, however. He reminds us of what Jesus said and did (John 14:26). But since what Jesus said and did is an infinite treasure, the Holy Spirit unwraps that treasure for us. Over the years, the church has seen more deeply into that treasure, and we have the development of what we call sacred tradition. But it also happens in our personal lives, as I will explore in the next chapter.

....

Lord Jesus, what incredible riches you have given us in your Holy Spirit! I need fear nothing, for divine power, the Paraclete, is at my side, no matter what challenges I may face. I beg you, prepare my heart for a new outpouring of that Spirit that will give me wisdom when I speak. May he also enlighten my mind and inflame my heart to understand and treasure more and more all the gifts you have given me. Amen.

Chapter 11

Revealer

In the previous chapter, we approached the theme of the Holy Spirit as revealer. The Paraclete is the number-one witness to Jesus, but he also teaches us about him. Here we would like to explore further that aspect of the Holy Spirit as revealer.

The first revealer, of course, was Jesus himself. The long poem by which John introduces his gospel ends this way: "No one has ever seen God. The Only-Begotten, who is God, ever in the Father's bosom, has revealed him" (John 1:18). This verse lifts the curtain on the public life of Jesus, beginning with the witness of John the Baptist. The Letter to the Hebrews begins similarly, by recalling how God spoke long ago and in many ways through the prophets but has now spoken to us in his Son (Hebrews 1:1-4). St. Paul also begins his letter to the Romans the same way, stressing that the resurrection was the full revelation of Jesus as Son of God (Romans 1:1-4). If the resurrection of Jesus revealed the power of God, then the death of Jesus on the cross revealed the love of God: "He loved me and gave himself up for me" (Galatians 2:20). Paul reminded the Galatians that he had portrayed before their eyes Christ crucified (3:1). In his first letter to the Corinthians, he likewise proclaimed Christ crucified, but he also told them that mere human knowledge or wisdom could not grasp such a mystery (1:18-25). Only the Holy Spirit could do that (2:6-16).

All this makes clear that there are two steps in God's plan of revelation: first, the historical events of Jesus' birth, death and resurrection; and second, the gift of the Holy Spirit in the believer. The first is the external revelation; the second is the internal. For example, you and I could learn the facts about Jesus, and we could study the witness to those facts in the New Testament, the writings of the first believers in Jesus. But we could do that as we might study any other subject—archaeology, for example. Such an endeavor would give us information but not transformation. Transformation happens when I experience those external events as addressed to me and when I let them change me. That is the work of the Holy Spirit. He is the internal revealer, the personalizer of the word, moving the message from the head to the heart and to the will, enabling us to say, "Yes, that is true. That is God speaking to me. I repent of my sins. I 'was blind but now I see.'"

The moment of conversion is only the beginning of what I see. Paul expresses this revealing role of the Holy Spirit in this way:

What eye has not see, and ear has not heard,
   And what has not occurred to the human heart,
The wonders God has prepared for those who love him,
These God has revealed to us through the Spirit.
(1 Corinthians 2:9-10)

Paul goes on to explain how this happens: "For the Spirit explores all things, even the depths of God" (1 Corinthians 2:10b). Whenever I read this line, I think of the discovery of the

Titanic, particularly the moment when, with the help of deep-water searchlights and cameras, the explorers got their first view of the fabled ship. What a revelation that was! The lights and the camera explored the depths. That's what the Holy Spirit does with the depths of God! God's depths are infinite, so there is no end to the exploring, but the Holy Spirit reveals more and more of the deep mysteries of God. He begins by revealing to us all that is contained in what we call the paschal mystery—the whole mystery of Christ. And through the mystery of Christ, he leads us to the mystery of the Trinity.

Why is the Spirit capable of revealing this to us? Because he is God's own Spirit: "For who knows what pertains to a human person, if not that person's own spirit? Similarly, no one knows the things of God except the Spirit of God. Now we have not received the spirit of the world but the Spirit from God, that we may know the gifts God has given us" (1 Corinthians 2:11-12). When you stop to think about it, isn't this unspeakable? The Holy Spirit empowers us with a supernatural faculty for seeing into the very heart of God. This is not just the kind of awe we might experience in gazing at the universe, nor is it the kind of "eureka" feeling a scientist might experience in making a new discovery, nor the kind of excitement astronaut Neil Armstrong experienced when he stepped on the moon. We are seeing God as he sees himself—partially, of course, but also really. And that is the amazing work of the Holy Spirit. Of course, we are speaking of the truths that are expressed in our creedal formulas, but we are also speaking about the experience of those truths as life-giving light in prayer. The Titanic explorers were told by their instruments that the ship was below them. But they didn't see it until the camera showed it to their eyes. So we can know the truths of the faith and even believe in them intellectually, but only the Holy Spirit can turn on the lights and give us an experience of their wonders.

Insight into What Is Revealed

There is a word in the letters of Paul for this illumination. It's the Greek word *epignosis*. It means a specific kind of knowledge, akin to recognition. When Ulysses eventually returned home, he wondered if his father would "recognize" him. When Peter escaped from prison and knocked on the door of the Christian home, Rhoda "recognized" his voice. (Acts 12:13-14). Recognition thus supposes a prior knowledge of the person or the object. In the letters of the New Testament, especially those of Paul, the word always meant a religious knowledge, and when Paul prayed for his readers to grow in knowledge, the best translation is "insight." The Holy Spirit gives us an insight into what is revealed.

The knowledge that is revealed has an aspect of continuity and also one of discontinuity. Continuity, because it is the same God who reveals through his Holy Spirit—and the object is the same, the mystery of his revelation in Christ. Discontinuity, because there is a surprising revelation of something new in the mystery, a new understanding of some aspect of it. That this unfolding knowledge is a gift of the Spirit appears from the fact that most often the word appears in Paul's prayers. "I never cease giving thanks for you as I remember you in my prayers, that the God of our Lord Jesus Christ will give you a *spirit* of wisdom and revelation in *knowledge* of him" (Ephesians 1:17). "My prayer is that your love may more and more abound in *knowledge (insight)*" (Philippians 1:9). "We do not cease praying . . . that you be filled with *insight* into his will, in all *spiritual* wisdom and understanding . . . growing in the *knowledge* of God" (Colossians 1:9-10). "That their hearts be united in love . . . leading to *insight* into the mystery of God, Christ, in whom are all the treasures of wisdom and knowledge" (Colossians 2:2-3).

For us, it means that we must pray for this insight, as Paul did for his readers. This can happen in our personal prayer, but it can also happen at a prayer meeting, either through the gift of prophecy or through individuals sharing their insights into the Scriptures, making the word fresh and active. Whenever we give a talk about the Lord, we should ask for the kind of insight that will make the word come alive, both for ourselves and those who hear us.

....

Lord, help me to realize that in you I have found a store of endless treasures. Grant that I may be docile to the Holy Spirit, who wishes to reveal to me more and more of your riches, that I may praise you for who you are, for what you have done, and for what you continue to do. May I come to understand my faith better, and may I also taste what I believe in, that I may grow daily in union with you and be a channel of your light to others. Amen.

Chapter 12

Promise

The couple standing before me was nervous, and it didn't help that in their tux and bridal gown, they faced the lurking threat of boutonniere drooping or train misbehaving. But here they both were, ready to pronounce their marriage vows. I was amazed, as I always am at weddings, when each of the two young people dares to reach into their entire unknown future, grab it, and give it away in a single sentence. I am reminded of a wedding that took place beneath a Lenten banner that happened to dominate the sanctuary, which proclaimed, "Father, forgive them, they don't know what they are doing." And yet that foolish abandonment of one to the other is precisely the beauty of weddings. It is also why the church surrounds it with the strength of a sacrament, because faithful love is more divine than human. The promised and the given future—that's what a wedding is all about.

But I see another couple in front of me. They come forward not with triumphal wedding march but slowly, leaning on each other as they mount the altar steps. No white gown or sleek tux for them, but a suit and a dress they have worn on festive occasions for the last ten years. They are about to renew their wedding vows for the fiftieth time. If there was beauty and awe when they promised their future a half century earlier, what beauty and awe there is now that those promises have been fulfilled!

The beauty of promises made. The beauty of promises kept.

On August 15, 1947, an eighteen-year-old George Montague, along with twenty other young men, knelt before his provincial and pronounced his first vows as a Marianist religious. His uncle had told him he was too young to know his own mind. But as I write this, I am celebrating my sixtieth year of faithful love. God knows that it is his faithful love rather than my own.

The grace of promises made. The grace of promises kept.

God makes promises and keeps them. That could be the subtitle of the Bible. God promised Abraham land and descendants. Abraham believed God, and the Lord confirmed his promise with a covenant ritual and an external sign. The Lord told Abraham to cut animals in half and lay them out as if forming a path. This was one of the ways people made covenants in those days. Each party would walk through the halves and say, "May my god and your god do this to me and worse yet, if I do not keep what I promise." As a testimony of his covenant promise to Abraham, the Lord then passed like a fire through the halves (Genesis 15:1-21), but he did not require Abraham to do so. God is going to keep his promise, come what may. But that covenant ritual was passing. The Lord gave Abraham another sign of the covenant, a more permanent one: circumcision. From one generation to the next, it would be a sign of God's promise to his people.

Despite all their infidelities over the centuries, God kept his promises. Abraham's descendants multiplied and eventually entered the promised land. But there, the motley tribes needed protection against the Philistines and others, so the Lord gave them a king, Saul first and then David. To King David, the Lord made another promise, a startling one, through the prophet

Nathan: David's dynasty would last forever (2 Samuel 7:11-16). The prophecy was not perfectly fulfilled in the history of Israel; the dynasty ceased temporarily, when because of the people's sins, Jeremiah said, the Babylonians took them into exile. But when the angel appeared to Mary at the annunciation, he said that her son would "rule over the house of Jacob forever, and of his kingdom there will be no end" (Luke 1:33). Jesus would be the promised Messiah-King who would reign forever—there would be no other king than he on the throne of David. Peter said that the enthronement of Jesus as this everlasting king happened when, having died, Jesus was raised up and seated at the right hand of the Father, who proclaimed him Lord and Messiah (Acts 2:36). So the risen Lord Jesus is the ultimate fulfillment of the promise made to Abraham and to David.

A Promise Fulfilled

But there is more. God had also promised to pour out his Spirit on all his people: "I will pour out water upon the thirsty ground and streams on the dry land. I will pour out my spirit on your descendants and my blessing on your offspring" (Isaiah 44:3). And even more specifically, "I will pour out my spirit on all mankind. Your sons and daughters will prophesy, your old men dream dreams, your young men see visions. Even on the servants and handmaids in those days, I will pour out my spirit" (Joel 2:28-29). Peter quoted this text to explain what had happened in the upper room. The Holy Spirit who was promised long ago had now been sent, and the explosion of tongues and prophecy bore witness to it.

This was not only promised by the Father in the Old Testament, it was also repeated by Jesus before his ascension. Luke reported this twice, once at the end of his gospel ("I am sending upon you the promise of my Father, but stay in the city until you are clothed with power from on high," Luke 24:49) and again at the beginning of the Acts of the Apostles ("He told them not to depart from Jerusalem but to wait for the promise of the Father that I told you about. For John baptized with water, but in a few days you will be baptized with the Holy Spirit," Acts 1:4-5).

St. Paul also spoke of the Holy Spirit as God's promise fulfilled. He saw the promise of descendents fulfilled in Jesus and in all who believe (Galatians 3:7, 16-17). What of the land? The New Testament does not speak of Palestine as the fulfillment of that part of the Old Testament promise to Abraham. Instead, the Letter to the Hebrews speaks of heaven as the ultimate home and place of rest (4:1-11). And Paul speaks of the Holy Spirit, already a beginning of what is to come (2 Corinthians 1:22; Ephesians 1:14). The Holy Spirit is the fulfillment of the land-promise made to Abraham. Or so it seems from Galatians 3:14, where Paul says that the law is now bypassed, so that "the blessing of Abraham might be extended to the Gentiles through Christ Jesus, so that we might receive the promise of the Spirit through faith." In the section that speaks of Christ as the fulfillment of the promise of descendents, Paul does not mention the land, the second part of the promise; instead, he speaks of the Holy Spirit. The land, then, was only a preparation for a greater gift: the Holy Spirit, and ultimately heaven.

A Further Promise

The Holy Spirit, then, is not only the fulfillment of a promise, he is a further promise, a further assurance of God's fidelity. In 2 Corinthians 1:20-22 Paul says that all the promises of God have found their "Yes," that is, their fulfillment, in Christ, God's Anointed One, "and he has anointed us too, and has put his seal on us and deposited the Spirit in our hearts as the first installment." The first installment is not merely a promise of more to come, it is the beginning of it. In traditional Mexican weddings, the groom gives his bride a bag of coins called *arras* (a word derived from the Greek *arrabon,* meaning first installment), as his pledge to support her for the rest of her life. The Holy Spirit is the *arras,* the beginning with more to come. Or, let us suppose a father promises his ten-year-old daughter that he will pay her college tuition. He gives his word. But suppose he goes to the college that very day and makes a first payment toward the tuition. That is what God has done for us.

He has not only promised eternal life, he has given us the beginning of it in the Holy Spirit. In Ephesians 1:13-14 the promise, the Holy Spirit, and the first installment are all wrapped together: "You heard the word of truth, the gospel of your salvation. You believed in it and were sealed with the *Holy Spirit, the promise, the first installment* of our inheritance." The Greek of this sentence can be translated in different ways. The New American Bible and the New International Version translate it as "the promised Holy Spirit," understanding the Holy Spirit as the fulfillment of the promise of the Old Testament and of Jesus. But the literal translation is "the Holy Spirit *of* the

101

promise." This could be what the scholars call an "epexegetic genitive," which simply means that "promise" is a synonym for "Holy Spirit," and that's the way I have translated it. We have something like that in English when we say "the city of Rome." We simply mean the city that is Rome. In this understanding, then, the Holy Spirit is not only the fulfillment of God's promise of old but also the promise of what is to come, and this is confirmed by what immediately follows: "the first installment of our inheritance." In other words, the promise, which is the Holy Spirit, points forward, but in a way that is more than a sign. The Holy Spirit is the beginning of heaven right now. Nowhere is this clearer than in 2 Corinthians 5:5, where Paul talks precisely about heaven as our destiny and then concludes, "He who has readied us for this very thing is God, who has given us the Spirit as the first installment." Elsewhere Paul called the Holy Spirit the firstfruits (Romans 8:23).

The Letter to the Hebrews brings this reality even closer to our experience. The word of God there says we have already *tasted* the heavenly gift and shared in the Holy Spirit (6:4). When you were a child, and your mother was mixing the dough to bake a cake, did she ever let you lick the spoon? My mother did. And when I licked it, I wanted more, though I would have to wait till dinner. But I already knew what it tasted like!

All these figures come down to the same awesome truth: the Holy Spirit is heaven in our hearts, here and now. Not the fullness, of course, but the Holy Spirit in heaven is no different from the Holy Spirit in us now. Even as I write this, I am overwhelmed by the reality. Paul said it over and over: the Holy Spirit is the real beginning of the life of the blessed in heaven.

And, of course, as we saw in the chapter on Gift, the Holy Spirit is not a thing, not an idea, not even a feeling. The Holy Spirit is a person, the divine Person who is the mutual love of the Father and the Son. So with the Holy Spirit, we also have the Father and the Son.

Recently, off the coast of Columbia, some English explorers discovered a sixteenth-century sunken ship that contained gold coins worth billions of dollars. We have in the depth of our hearts a treasure worth far more. The explorers had to work hard to find their treasure. All we have to do is long for it and ask for it.

....

O Holy Spirit, you are the Father's promise fulfilled. But you are also the beginning of the "not yet." Open my eyes so that I may see the treasure that you are, long for you in my heart more and more, and embrace you with my entire being. Amen.

Chapter 13

Abba

In 1974 the prisoners of war were returning home from North Vietnam. Colonel Robert Stirm had been taken captive early in the war, and his wife, two sons, and two daughters had not seen him in six years. When he landed at Travis Air Force Base in California, a photographer caught the moment as he was walking down the tarmac and his family was running toward him. Running. Of the ten feet among them, only two were visible on the ground. The pack was being led by Stirm's mini-skirted sixteen-year-old daughter, platforms airborne, eyes agog, arms flung wide. One can imagine the next moment, when she cried, "Daddy!" and fell into his embrace.

St. Paul tells us that this is what the Holy Spirit does for us: we are God's children, and we cry out, "*Abba!* Father!" (Romans 8:15; Galatians 4:6). Paul chooses the Greek word *kradzo* for crying out, which even sounds like a shout, to suggest the deep-felt, excited love that gives birth to the cry. It was love that sped the family to their husband and father and love that fired the embrace. So, too, it is the Holy Spirit, love in person, who leads us to acclaim God as our Father.

How would we even know that God is *Abba*? Look at the world around you. Put aside the atheists and the agnostics. Then look at the world of those who identify themselves as believers. Some are polytheists, some are animists, some worship the earth, some simply acknowledge some kind of superior power, personal or not ("the Force be with you"). Muslims believe in a personal God, the creator, but their sense of his otherness keeps them from giving him a more intimate title. Practicing Jews believe in the God of history who intervened to save his people, and yes, they call him Father, but only about a dozen times in the Old Testament, and it is always the formal title, "Father." But *Abba* is more intimate than that. It is the kind of address we use familiarly with our "Dad," "Daddy," or "Papa." That is the daring intimacy Christians have been given by the Holy Spirit with the all-holy God. But where do we get that name for God?

From Jesus. And where did *he* get it? Growing up in an observant Jewish family who attended the synagogue every Sabbath, he heard all the Old Testament titles for God: Lord, King, Mighty One, Rock, Fortress, Shepherd, Deliverer, and yes, Father. But none of those names struck him as adequate to express his experience of God. Not that any name would ever be adequate for the immensity of God, but Jesus did have an experience that came as close as human language could express. It was not in the synagogue that he learned it. It was in the home and workshop of Joseph that he found it. The first person Jesus called *Abba* was Joseph. And when, as Jesus grew in wisdom, age, and grace (Luke 2:52), he came to name his own experience of God, he could find no better human title than the one he had first given to Joseph. What this says about the vocation of fatherhood is immense, and it would take an entire book to adequately explore it. Suffice it to say that the father is the first to give the child an inkling of what God might be: loving, strong, faithful, wise, ever calling the child to grow and flourish. (I will deal with the question of the mother's influence later.)

It was Jesus' intimate experience of God that kept the name *Abba* on his lips throughout his public life. In the Gospel of Matthew alone, the name "Father" for God appears 44 times, and in the Gospel of John, 115 times. Jesus never addresses God otherwise. In Mark's account of Jesus' prayer in his agony in the garden, the evangelist Mark interrupts the flow of his Greek script to write the Aramaic *Abba:* "*Abba,* Father, all things are possible for you. Let this cup pass from me; but not what I will but what you will" (Mark 14:36). Paul, too, writing in Greek to his Greek-speaking communities, repeats the very Aramaic word Jesus used. But Paul tells us that this name is more than a souvenir from Jesus' life. To cry *Abba* from our hearts, to meet the Father in our personal or community prayer, we can do so only through the prompting of the Holy Spirit. "Because you are sons, God has sent the Spirit of his Son into our hearts, crying, '*Abba!* Father!'" (Galatians 4:6). And in Romans 8:14-15: "Those who are led by the Spirit of God are sons of God. For you have not received the spirit of slavery that leads you back into fear, but you have received the Spirit of sonship in whom we cry: '*Abba!* Father!'"

Several things are remarkable about these two texts. First, they are Trinitarian, the first explicitly so, the second implicitly (because we are sons in the Son). Second, it is the role of the Holy Spirit to disclose the Father to us. And third, it is the Spirit who not only enables us to cry "*Abba!*" but who actually does it. Through the Holy Spirit, Jesus shares with us his own experience of the Father!

The disciples had seen Jesus pray many times. One day, after they had watched him pray, they asked him to teach them to pray. Jesus gave them the one prayer that marks every Christian, beginning, "[Our] Father *(Abba)*. . . ." After the prayer, Jesus gave an example of perseverance in prayer, the nagging neighbor who needs bread at night and finally gets it because of his persistence. So "Ask and you shall receive," Jesus concluded. And then he returned to the Father with whom this catechism on prayer began: "If you, though evil, know how to give good gifts to your children, how much more will the Father in heaven give the Holy Spirit to those who ask him" (Luke 11:13). The connection of the conclusion with the beginning of the passage is intentional. Jesus' answer to the disciples' request to teach them to pray was more than the Our Father. It was this whole section (Luke 11:1-13), and that last verse amounts to saying this: "I have given you the words to pray, but you will not experience what they mean without the Holy Spirit. The Holy Spirit will teach you interiorly what the words say exteriorly. And you can have the Holy Spirit for the asking, because the Father wants to give him to you more than you want to receive him."

Healing the "Father Wound"

But now, let's be honest. How many really care about knowing God as Father? Few fathers we have known even come close to looking like St. Joseph. If your father was the strong, loving, caring person that came close to looking like the saint, how blessed you are! But in our world today, the absent or abusive or neglectful father is fairly common—as I know from the many men and women who have come to me for help in healing their "father wound." That wound is most often at the root of other problems, too.

I have had to deal with my own father wound. My father, whom I have already described as a six-foot-tall, boot- and Stetson-wearing 280-pound rancher, was a good man, a very good man—honest, fair, outgoing, willing to help those in need. He had a sense of humor woven into the story-telling mantle that had fallen to him from his Irish ancestors. He was devout in an observant, pre–Vatican II way—saying his rosary during Sunday Mass as his way of accompanying the Latin he didn't understand. And every night before retiring, he would kneel at his bed and pray. He loved his sons, all five of us, with a love that, as happens with many fathers, spurned affection for action. (Our mother made up for that.)

But he had a temper. Patriarch that he was, when his temper flared, the house shook. And so I had a fear of him. Coupled with that fear was the feeling that he wanted me to be more than I could be. I was pigeon-toed when I walked, and he would often shout at me, sometimes when visitors were around, "George, walk straight!" I couldn't help it; I was born that way. Is it any wonder that when I learned the Our Father, I thought of Papa instead?

The healing of my father wound was a slow process. Other father figures came into my life, and thanks to them, my father image was broadened. After joining the Marianists, I began to see, through prayer, that I was burdening God with my father's baggage. But the defining moment of the change happened when I was prayed over for the baptism in the Holy Spirit on Christmas

Eve 1970. The Holy Spirit made me cry *Abba!* How can I explain what it is like to shed crippling fear and realize that I am loved by a Father who is nothing but love, who has all the wonderful traits of my earthly father, yet without the limitations that made me fear him? God put me on a journey that led ultimately to a forty-day retreat experience. There, I met my earthly father in prayer and said all the things I couldn't tell him while he was alive, and then, believing that he, too, now saw everything in the light of God, fancied what he would want to say to me. That prayer happened at midnight, but it was sunrise in my heart.

I am so grateful to the Holy Spirit for leading me into the depths of *Abba,* depths that he continues to reveal to me. And I pray for those who are still hurting from their father wound, and especially for those who feel that they must simply do away with fatherhood because of their negative experiences with their earthly fathers, or with men in general, for that matter. That is not the way of freedom and wholeness. *Abba* is.

....

Abba, Father, Jesus said that to know you is eternal life (John 17:3), and you have given us that life already now, though in the obscurity of faith. Fill me once again with your Holy Spirit, that I may be able to cry Abba! and know your fatherly embrace with that perfect love that casts out fear and empowers me with the very strength of your Son. Amen.

Chapter 14

Jesus

It may seem strange that we would dedicate a chapter to Jesus in this book, since we have been talking about him all along. Indeed, the Holy Spirit is inseparable from Jesus, but precisely for this reason we need to ask the Holy Spirit, our explorer of the depths of God (1 Corinthians 2:10), to shine his light on our blessed Lord. How is the Holy Spirit related to Jesus?

On the one hand, the Holy Spirit proves his authenticity by bearing witness to Jesus (Revelation 19:10). If anyone claims to have the Holy Spirit, or any other spirit for that matter, but either denies Jesus or says that there is an alternative way to God, he or she is certainly not inspired by the Holy Spirit. On the other hand, anyone who truly believes in Jesus and confesses that he is Lord and that God raised him from the dead (Romans 10:9) can do so only by the power of the Holy Spirit: "No one speaking in the Spirit can say 'Cursed be Jesus,' and no one can say 'Jesus is Lord' except by the Holy Spirit" (1 Corinthians 12:3).

The first situation looks at Jesus from the viewpoint of the Spirit of prophecy, of the claim to direct inspiration. People might not say "Cursed be Jesus," but today there are folk healers (known as *curanderos* and *curanderas* in Spanish), palm readers, fortune tellers, psychics, and a litany of other hawkers of knowledge or salvation, who might even toss a dash of Jesus into their mix to draw the unwary—but this is not the Holy Spirit! You can tell the Holy Spirit by his fidelity to Jesus and to his word and to the church he established to continue his work.

The second situation looks at the Spirit from the viewpoint of Jesus. Whoever says, "Jesus is Lord" (the earliest Christian creed), can do so only in the power of the Holy Spirit. Whoever truly believes in Jesus and strives to live his faith can take consolation that he or she already possesses the Holy Spirit in that very act of faith. In fact, conversion itself is a gift of the Holy Spirit, for it is the grace of the Holy Spirit that draws us to Jesus. A fire in the fireplace already attracts us and begins to warm us before we get to it. At the moment we choose to come in out of the cold and approach the fire, the fire is already at work. Although the Holy Spirit may explode dramatically later in life, the seed is already planted there by faith. That means that if you believe in Jesus and give your life to him, you have the Holy Spirit.

Of course, the Holy Spirit may not have you yet in the fullness he would like to give you. In Texas we have a plant called the *agave*, which has heavy, spiny-margined leaves that prefer the ground to the heights. The popular name for the plant is "the century plant" because, for twenty years or so, it will just sit there with apparently nothing to do, until one day it seems to come alive and shoots up a staff to a height of thirteen or fourteen feet, topped with a crown of yellow flowers. With me, that's the way the Holy Spirit was—latent, hardly noticed, and nevertheless there, until some brothers and sisters prayed over me for the baptism in the Holy Spirit. The century plant bloomed!

St. Augustine spoke of the awakening of a grace earlier received. Today we might think of that concept in terms of a time-release capsule. The effects of that kind of pill may take place later than when it is first swallowed. So it is with the Holy Spirit.

There is an important behavioral consequence to this fact. If you ask a Christian—or worse yet, if you ask a priest—if he or she is "Spirit-filled," you are asking for trouble. The question will be confusing to anyone who has already professed faith in Jesus and who says in the Creed, "I believe in the Holy Spirit." And it will be especially confusing to a priest to whom the ordaining bishop has said, "Receive the Holy Spirit." The person may even be insulted and think you are claiming to be "holier than thou." A religious sister who was a director of novices once asked to see me. I hadn't asked her (God forbid!) if she was "Spirit-filled." But my excitement about the Holy Spirit troubled her. "You're saying that you are holier than I am," she said. "No," I replied, "I'm saying the Holy Spirit has made *me* different from what *I* was." The truth is that your fellow Christian and your priest already have the Holy Spirit. Maybe they haven't experienced him yet the way you have. Know that the best way to draw others to the baptism in the Holy Spirit is simply to show by your life (and maybe occasionally by your words) what it has done for you. Then maybe they will feel a twinge of holy envy to want what you've got. That's the way I was won over—I saw the fruits in others, and I wanted what they had. God gave me the grace to realize that just being baptized and confirmed and ordained did not mean that I was living in the full power of the Holy Spirit.

I have learned that one way to spell the name of God is M-O-R-E, and that I can never have enough of the Holy Spirit. Even as I write this, I am aware that if I rest satisfied with where

I am, I am not being docile to the Holy Spirit, who is constantly leading. I am not experiencing the wonders of being God's son, because only "those who are *led* by the Spirit of God are sons of God" (Romans 8:14). I have often wondered about that text of St. Paul. Can't you be a child of God without being led by the Spirit? Do I have to respond to every movement of the Holy Spirit to be a child of God? I'm sure that Paul didn't quite mean it that way. What he did mean, surely, was that the movement of the Spirit in me reminds me that I am God's child and that responding to this particular movement would confirm once again who I am. To move in the Spirit is to act as God's child. The Father does not, however, remove our free will, so that it is possible not only to resist or neglect the gentle movement of the Spirit but even to grieve him through sin (Ephesians 4:30).

Pope John Paul II said that upon rising each morning, he would pray that he would respond to every inspiration of the Holy Spirit that day. When he was a boy, his father had given him a morning prayer to the Holy Spirit, which he said to his dying day.

The Spirit Moved Jesus

We have already seen several biblical instances of Jesus as the *source* of the Holy Spirit (giver of living water, water from the rock, Jesus' promise to send the Holy Spirit, the river flowing from the throne of God and the Lamb). But there is another dimension we have not explored: the Spirit moving Jesus himself. Mark relates that after Jesus' baptism, the Spirit *drove* him into the desert (Mark 1:12). The Greek verb Mark chose is almost violent. It is elsewhere used to throw someone overboard, even to cast out demons. Certainly Mark wanted to suggest that the movement of the Holy Spirit was compelling for Jesus. He *had* to go into the desert. Matthew's language is softer, saying Jesus was *led* into the desert by the Spirit (4:1), as does Luke (4:1). Luke gives the Spirit even more attention by saying that Jesus was "filled with the Holy Spirit" and by suggesting that the Spirit not only led Jesus in the desert but stayed with him there: "Jesus, filled with the Holy Spirit, returned from the Jordan and was led by the Spirit in the desert" (4:1). The imperfect tense could be translated "was being led," the sense being that during the entire forty days in the desert, Jesus was led by the Holy Spirit as he battled with the devil. Later, when the seventy-two disciples returned from their mission with great success in casting out demons, Jesus said, "I saw Satan falling like lightning from the sky" (Luke 10:18). And Jesus "rejoiced in the Holy Spirit and said, 'I praise you, Father, Lord of Heaven and earth'" (Luke 10:21). The success of the disciples was a replay of Jesus' victory in the Holy Spirit over Satan in the desert.

Most important, Jesus was conceived by the Holy Spirit (Luke 1:35). The miracle of the incarnation was the work of the Holy Spirit with the cooperation of Mary, so the Holy Spirit was in a sense woven into the very constitution of Jesus' person. And why not? Jesus is from all eternity the Son embraced by the Father in the love of the Holy Spirit. That is why Paul could say that Jesus was descended from David according to the flesh "but was installed as Son of God in power according to the Spirit of holiness through resurrection from the dead" (Romans 1:3-4). The expression "Spirit of holiness" is probably an early Jewish, pre-Pauline way of referring to the Holy Spirit, contrasting with "according to the flesh" in the previous line. By his resurrection, Jesus became a "life-giving spirit" (1 Corinthians 15:45), but he first received the Holy Spirit in his humanity from the Father before pouring it out on the church (Acts 2:33).

All this suggests not only that Jesus is the source of the Holy Spirit but that we can observe Jesus to learn how to live daily under the direction and guidance of the Holy Spirit. Luke especially would have us understand that every word and action of Jesus was a revelation of the Holy Spirit and an example to us of how to live the Spirit-led life. But imitation of Jesus is only part of our call. By the power of the Holy Spirit, we are being transformed into his risen image from one degree of glory to another (2 Corinthians 3:18).

....

Lord Jesus, I worship and adore you. Help me to keep my eyes on you, the forerunner and finisher of our faith (Hebrews 12:2), as I seek to imitate you. But as I do, transform me into your glorious image by the power of your Holy Spirit. Amen.

Chapter 15

Mary

As I was growing up, my family could have said, with the disciples of John the Baptist whom Paul discovered at Ephesus, "We haven't even heard that there is a Holy Spirit" (Acts 19:2). But we were spared a total aridity because we knew someone who, without our realizing it, was filtering the Holy Spirit to us. It was Mary. Somehow in this woman we were given some inkling of who or what the Holy Spirit is.

My father had come back from Lourdes at the end of his service in the First World War with a deep devotion to this "lovely lady dressed in blue." And that devotion was anchored firmly by what happened to his first son, Frank, at the age of two. In my grandparents' farmhouse, a kettle of water was boiling in the open fireplace when Frank, in an unnoticed moment of curiosity, reached and tipped the kettle over on himself, severely scalding his little leg. So severe was the burn that it demanded a skin graft. One of the ranch hands offered to undergo the operation to provide the skin. But our Aunt Margaret, before putting Frank to bed the night before the operation, sprinkled some Lourdes water on the wound and prayed devoutly that the Lady of Lourdes would intercede for a miracle. The next morning, the skin was so well recovered that no graft was needed. That healing obviously made an impact on our family, especially on my father.

This kind of activation of faith through signs is the work of the Holy Spirit, but often he stays in the background and works through human instruments. Of these, after Jesus, his favorite seems to be Mary. And why not? She was his chosen vessel to achieve the miracle of miracles, the virginal conception and birth, in time, of the Son of God. Often called spouse of the Holy Spirit, Mary embodies the feminine face of God, which is sometimes attributed to the Holy Spirit. I remember taking a walk with a young man in Lithuania whose English was adequate but not perfect. Whenever he would speak of the Spirit, he would use "her" or "she," because in Lithuanian "spirit" is feminine! It was a refreshing reminder that God is beyond the conceptual metaphors of our language, even when those metaphors are the ones he chose by which to reveal himself!

The Holy Spirit "overshadowed" Mary, enabling her to conceive Jesus. We discussed the metaphor of the cloud in an earlier chapter, so we simply need to recall here that the word is taken from the story of the cloud overshadowing the tabernacle in the desert, a sign of the divine presence. We can conclude that if Jesus is the Word made flesh by the power of the Holy Spirit, Mary is the living tabernacle of the Word, made so in the very same action of the Spirit.

Mary is the Model Responder

Even prior to conceiving Jesus, Mary was moved by the Holy Spirit to give her yes to the mystery, and so she became the model, the prototype of obedient response to God's plan of salvation for all ages to come. In fact, it is this obedient response, even more than her physical mothering of Jesus, that is heralded in the gospels. For while the divine motherhood is unique, responding to the word is something all are called to do, and fortunately in this we have Mary to learn from. She is blessed twice for her yes, first by Elizabeth, who exclaimed, "Blessed is she who believed that the words spoken to her by the Lord would be fulfilled" (Luke 1:45). And later, when a woman from the crowd cried out, "Blessed is the womb that bore you and the breasts at which you nursed," Jesus replied, "Rather, blessed are those who hear the word of God and obey it" (Luke 11:27-28).

So the Holy Spirit worked in Mary not only the unspeakable mystery of the incarnation, but also gave her the privilege of being the first, the ideal, and the model responder to God's revealed plan. In other words, she who received the Word of God in her womb also received the word of God in her heart, from where we might learn to receive. Both receptions were the work of the Holy Spirit. Jesus might be rejected by the temple priests and the Pharisees, he might be betrayed by a friend, he might be denied by his own chief disciple and abandoned by the rest to be crucified by the Romans, but he did have one heart that gave a perfect and persevering welcome to him: his mother.

Those who fear that drawing close to Mary will lead them away from Jesus have not understood the entire trinitarian foundation of the Christian faith. To look at the Father is to see the Son. To look at the Son is to see the Father. To look at the Holy Spirit is to be thrown into the mutual embrace of Father and Son. The Trinity is about relationships, about the self that is constituted by the total gift to and from the other. And relationships are what God's work in time and history is all about, too. To look into Mary's eyes is to see Jesus, for he is all she cares about. And who better than a mother can teach us to love her Son?

The Cloud may overshadow the sanctuary, but the Cloud also moves on—and so does the sanctuary. Mary will move with the Cloud. Model listener, she heard the entire message, not merely that she was to be mother of the Messiah (who could not have been overwhelmed with that mission?), but also that her cousin Elizabeth was six months pregnant, and that meant that Elizabeth would be in need. The Holy Spirit did not sculpt Mary into a statue to await pilgrimages; rather, he moved her into service, with haste, Luke says (1:39), foreshadowing the mission of the child she carried in her womb, who did not come to be served but to serve (Mark 10:45). At Elizabeth's door, Mary's voice of greeting triggered two events: the child in Elizabeth's womb leaped for joy, and Elizabeth was filled with the Holy Spirit (Luke 1:41, 44). Oh, if only I could just once hear the voice of Mary, I, too, would be filled with the Holy Spirit; I would leap for joy, and I could not contain my praise.

Neither could Elizabeth. The Holy Spirit moved her to cry out, "Blessed are you among women, and blessed is the fruit of your womb" (Luke 1:42). Through Elizabeth, the Holy Spirit gave future generations the words with which to praise Mary and her Son. Mary responded with her own song of thanksgiving and praise, the Magnificat. Luke does not have to tell us that the Holy Spirit led Mary to do this, for she was already filled with the Holy Spirit. In urgent need, the Spirit will move us to serve. But there is also an urgency to praise in the heart of one touched by the Holy Spirit. That happened at Pentecost, when the Holy Spirit transformed a group of fearful disciples into a community singing a symphony of praise (Acts 2:1-11). But it has already happened to Mary's extended family in this domestic Pentecost. While during Jesus' public ministry, we see only him empowered by the Holy Spirit—the disciples must wait (Luke 24:49)—here the Spirit poured himself out lavishly to Mary, to Elizabeth, to Zechariah when he prophesied at the birth of John (1:67), and to Simeon when Jesus was presented in the temple (2:25, 26).

A Domestic Pentecost

There is a great insight here for families. The outpouring of the Holy Spirit at Pentecost was followed by the powerful preaching of Peter and the explosive growth of the church through the missionary activity of the apostles and first disciples. But most fathers and mothers today are not called to the kind of proclamation we see in Acts. Their call and their gift is the domestic Pentecost, the visitation of the Holy Spirit within their own families, first and foremost in the simple types of relationships and services that we see in the extended family of Mary and Joseph. The Holy Spirit wishes to transform families into an earthly reflection of the holy Trinity. Divine bond of love, the Holy Spirit can do for families what is beyond their human powers of loving—bringing heaven to hearth and home.

But Mary is also associated with the Holy Spirit in the ongoing life of the church. Luke goes out of his way to mention that Mary joined the rest of the disciples in the upper room in expectant prayer for the coming of the Holy Spirit (Acts 1:14). Obviously, she who had already received the Holy Spirit would be the best mentor for how to receive the Spirit that Jesus had promised his disciples. In John's gospel, Jesus promises to send to his disciples "another Paraclete to be with you always, the Spirit of truth, whom the world cannot accept, because it neither sees him nor knows him. But you know him because he remains with you and will be in you. *I will not leave you orphans.* I will come to you" (John 14:16-18). In saying, "I will come to you," it is unlikely that Jesus was talking about his return to them in the resurrection appearances, because those were only temporary before he returned to his Father. Jesus must have been talking about the coming of the Paraclete, who would take his place. It is the Paraclete who would be the permanent "parent," assuring the disciples that they had not been orphaned. Jesus had called his disciples "little children" in John 13:33, as he spoke of his imminent departure. But now the "other Paraclete" would take over, not as an adoptive parent but as another way that Jesus would be with his own.

The Paraclete, however, is not visible as Jesus was. How would the spiritual parenting of the Paraclete be visible and tangible? We only have to turn to John 19:25-27 to find one way. Scholars generally agree that the beloved disciple at the foot of the cross stands for all the disciples who would now become Jesus' brothers and sisters (John 20:17). This is true not only because they have God as their Father but also because they have Mary as their mother. What Jesus said to the beloved disciple he also says to all who believe in him: "Behold your mother" (John 19:27). It is reasonable to think, then, that the union of Mary with the Holy Spirit from the moment of Jesus' conception has continued beyond the death and resurrection of Jesus: the Holy Spirit's spiritual parenting of the disciples finds it visible icon in Mary, mother of the disciples.

The word "paraclete" comes from the Greek verb *paraka-leo*. In the Greek text of Isaiah 66:7-13, the word is used to mean "to comfort," as it describes Jerusalem as a mother who comforts her children and through whom God himself comforts them. "As a mother comforts her child, so will I comfort you. In Jerusalem you will find your comfort" (verse 13). Seen from the New Testament perspective, the church is the new Jerusalem, and so is Mary, who is the church in her role as mother. Viewed in this way, the text can be read as fulfilled in the Holy Spirit, who comforts God's people through the gift of Mary, their mother.

....

Father, I deeply long for a new outpouring of your Holy Spirit in my life. Unworthy though I am, because of your love for me I know that you want to give me the Holy Spirit even more than I want to receive him. Jesus, your mother was present at the cross when you "handed over the Spirit." May she be at my side now as my mother, to show me how to receive this Gift of gifts. Amen.

Chapter 16

Power

A friend of mine in Florida was shopping for a used car for his wife. The dealer showed him a former police car in good condition, and he bought it. His wife enjoyed using it for her errands around town. One night she was driving home on a lonely country road, when the headlights of a pickup truck loomed behind her, tailing her uncomfortably close. Then the male driver swung around, passed her, and slowed down in front of her. She passed him, only to see him repeat the same move. When he did it a third time, she pressed her accelerator to the floor, swung past him and, much to her surprise, discovered her car rocketing ahead so fast that the pickup's headlights shrunk to a speck in her rearview mirror. Unknown to her, the car was armed with a police overtake gear. She had power she didn't know she had.

So do you when you receive the Holy Spirit. The Holy Spirit may have the gentleness of the dove; he may come as a quiet, delightful breeze or as refreshing water. But the Holy Spirit is also power. Jesus said as much: "You will receive *power* when the Holy Spirit comes upon you, and you will be my witnesses in Jerusalem, in all of Judea, in Samaria, and unto the ends of the earth" (Acts 1:8). The Greek word for power here is *dynamis*, from which we get our word "dynamite." So closely associated is the Holy Spirit with power that the words are practically interchangeable. Do you remember the time when Jesus was casting out a demon, and the Pharisees accused him of casting it out by Beelzebul, the prince of demons (Mark 3:22)? Jesus responded by saying that Satan may be the strongman, but Jesus is the stronger one who ties up the strongman and plunders his kingdom (3:27). And then Jesus said that the Pharisees had blasphemed against the Holy Spirit, because it was by the *power* of the Holy Spirit that Jesus cast out demons (3:29; Matthew 12:28). The angel told Mary, "The Holy Spirit will come upon you, and the *power* of the Most High will overshadow you" (Luke 1:35). Simon Magus, seeing that the Holy Spirit was given by the laying on of the apostles' hands, said, "Give me also this *power*" (Acts 8:18-19). Peter, preaching to the household of Cornelius, said, "God anointed Jesus with the Holy Spirit and *power*" (Acts 10:38). Paul prayed that the Romans "may be filled with hope in the *power* of the Holy Spirit" (Roman 15:13), and he spoke of what God had accomplished through him "by the power of signs and wonders, by the *power* of the Holy Spirit" (15:19).

You will note that most of these references to the Holy Spirit and power concern the charisms of healing and miracles, which we will speak about in a subsequent chapter. So, too, Paul recalled his first preaching to the Thessalonians, when "our gospel came to you not in word only but in *power* and the Holy Spirit" (1 Thessalonians 1:5). The contrast here with the preached word indicates that Paul's mission was accompanied by "signs and wonders," by miracles of some sort, worked by the Holy Spirit, confirming the truth of the gospel. He said the same thing in his first letter to the Corinthians: "My word and my preaching were not in persuasive words of wisdom but in a demonstration of spirit and *power*" (2:4).

More than Natural Power

So when the inspired authors of the New Testament identi-fied the Holy Spirit with power, they were simply saying that the Holy Spirit gives us the ability to do what we could not do by our natural gifts or strength. We can move in the power of God. Now, some people will think it presumptuous to say that human beings can operate on divine power. But if so, then the New Testament is presumptuous, for that is exactly what it is saying. As Christians, we are not expected to get along with only our natural powers. Our natural powers will not save us! Nor will our natural powers suffice for ministry. In this chapter, we will look at the power the Holy Spirit gives us to live the full Christian life. We will reflect on the charismatic, empowering gifts in the following chapters.

Sometimes it takes a crisis to get us to realize that we have power in the Holy Spirit that we didn't know we had. There is a story about some young frogs that were stuck in a deep muddy rut on a country road. Try as they might, over and over again, the frogs were unable to jump high enough to get out. Some older frogs came along and asked the younger ones what the trouble was. "We just can't get out. The walls of the hole are just too high." The older frogs said, "Sorry, we don't know how to help you," and they went on their way. About half an hour later, the old frogs returned, and the young frogs were sitting on the side of the road, smiling happily. "What happened?" the old frogs asked. "You said you couldn't get out of the hole." "That's right," said the young frogs, "but a big truck came along, and we had to!"

A crisis can be a blessing if it leads us to discover the power of the Holy Spirit. Jesus expected his disciples to run into crises. He told them that they would be dragged before governors and kings, but that they should not be anxious about how they were to speak or what they were to say, "for it will not be you who are speaking but the Spirit of your Father who is speaking in you" (Matthew 10:20).

Most of us will not be dragged before governors or kings. Our crises are far more typical: a problem we don't know how to handle, a dear one who has gotten into drugs, an alcoholic spouse, the loss of a job, or maybe depression or burnout. Burnout happened to me in the summer of 1968. A six-week vacation at the ranch helped, but the real turnaround—the discovery of new life and power—happened when I was prayed over for the baptism in the Holy Spirit two years later. Did the power come from the outside, or did it well up from the inside? It was obviously a gift, so in that sense it was new and so coming from the outside. But Jesus said that the Holy Spirit would be a fountain welling up from the inside, and that's exactly the way it felt when I was prayed over. Yes, brothers and sisters prayed over me from the outside, but the Holy Spirit welled up from the inside. I can only describe it as a bubbling up. However, the earlier crisis of burnout was itself a grace that put a cry in my heart, "My God, I need something!"

That something was power, but not the power of energy bars or antidepressants. It was the power of God's love inebriating me, of God telling me that he is my *Abba*. It was the power of joy. It was the power of falling in love. It was the power of being hugged and kissed by God.

That was nearly forty years ago. The exultation of those early days, like the romance of falling in love, would not last, but the power would. It would carry me through the tough times that lay ahead, all the valleys and deserts I would experience. That the Holy Spirit led Jesus into the desert after his baptism is significant. The vision of the split heavens and the dove may have passed, but the power had not. Jesus came forth from the battle fully tested. Satan had tested Jesus' entitlement by the Father as his Son, and Satan was blown away. I am sure that some of the weakening of my love-struck encounter with the Lord was due to infidelities on my part. But the rest of it was the kind of testing, of which Sirach speaks: "My son, when you come to serve the Lord, prepare yourself for trials" (2:1).

I certainly have not been tried, as so many early Christians were, to the shedding of my blood (Hebrews 12:4). In fact, I suspect the Lord knows that I'm too much of a sissy for him to try me with more than gnats around my face. But maybe, just maybe, the Holy Spirit inside has made the crosses lighter. Lighter, not sweeter. I'm not far enough along to call them sweeter, except for once by an exceptional grace when I was blasted for doing what I felt was God's work. People I've ministered to have been tried a lot more severely than I have been. A close friend of mine, the mother of six children, was confronted with a series of three tragedies. First, her husband walked out on her and their children to marry someone else. Then, one of her sons committed suicide. Within a month, a second son committed suicide. I was privileged to be beside her as she wept bitterly, but eventually she was able to say, "I want only what God wants." I heard in those words a *fiat*, a "let it be done," said by another woman overshadowed by the Spirit long ago. My friend had been baptized in the Holy Spirit and had a personal relationship with Jesus. The Holy Spirit bonded her with Mary at the foot of the cross, enabling both women to see through the windows of their tears a light in the night of their grief.

I have not spoken yet about the charismatic power of the Holy Spirit. I have spoken here of the empowerment to live the Christian life, to meet the challenges of daily life, whether these are the daily frustrations and annoyances or the bottom-falling-out crises that come our way. We might call this survival power. But God had more than our survival in mind when he gave us the Holy Spirit. He wants to make us missionaries, builders of his church and builders of his kingdom. That leads us to the next chapter.

....

Lord Jesus, thank you for the power you give me in the Holy Spirit. When trials come my way, remind me that with God all things are possible, that with the Holy Spirit I can scale any wall, and that in every situation I can win an overwhelming victory because of him who loved us (Romans 8:37). Amen.

Chapter 17

Gifts, Part I

Living water is spring water or river water that flows. Stagnant water has no outlets, while living water does. For the Holy Spirit to be truly alive in us, there must be outlets, and the Holy Spirit has provided them. These are the charisms of the Holy Spirit. "Charisms" means gifts, and these gifts of the Spirit are outlet gifts. We can say that the sacraments get the Holy Spirit *in*. The charisms get him *out*. To fully experience the living water of the Spirit, we need to yield to the charisms.

The first outlet gift is *praise*. The fire of the Holy Spirit at Pentecost turned the huddled community of the disciples into a blaze of praise. This praise did not consist in just reciting prayers or psalms of praise. It was so powerful that it broke the verbal barrier and gushed forth in tongues. That was the first sign that the Holy Spirit had truly come upon the community. So it is meant to be for us when we receive the Holy Spirit, who is the loving praise, the dance of the Father and the Son. We are moved to give our lips and our tongue over to the Holy Spirit so that his praise can flow through us.

But it is precisely there that many of us run into a brick wall. We want to receive the Holy Spirit, but we find it hard to let him out because we are unaccustomed to sounding like infants who babble and haven't learned to talk. This discomfort is understandable. Consider how important rational language is to us in our development. What a joy it was for our parents when we said our first word! And then we learned to say more words, then to speak in sentences, and then to write them. In elementary school, we learned how to write a paragraph. In high school or college, we learned how to write a term paper. Then, for the privileged, there is the master's degree, and finally, for some, the doctorate, when we write a dissertation that is the size of a book. Notice how our importance tends to be judged by how much mastery of the English language we have. Notice, too, that the more education we have, the greater the threat we will feel from going back to the preverbal stage of our infancy.

Of course, such babble would be foolish if we were trying to communicate with humans. But if we are trying to communicate with God, do we assume that God is more pleased with our finely honed words than with the sentiments of our hearts? Do we forget that Jesus said that unless we become like little children (Luke 18:15 says *infants*), we will not get into the kingdom of heaven? Well, here I was, with a doctorate and a handful of books published—and the Lord was inviting me to babble like a child. No way! I wanted to be as much in control as I had been of my thoughts and words in the books I had written. My theology degree had taught me to think critically. I even wanted to be in control of what my heart was saying to God. I thought it all had to go through the meat grinder of reason before it was presentable to him. But then even my reason told me that love doesn't work that way. A child loves long before he or she knows how to say, "I love you." And that, I came to realize through my study of St. Paul, is what the gift of tongues is. It amounts to saying, "God, you are too much for words!" We acknowledge that at certain moments in life, we are at a loss for words, such as when we are sharing someone's grief and we say to them, "I can't find words to say what I'm feeling." Then how can words ever be adequate to express what happens when we are kissed by God?

Going Beyond Reason

For adults, yielding to tongues may look and feel like going back to infancy. In fact, it is just the opposite. It is not going back before reason; it is going beyond it. It doesn't mean losing your mind and your ability to think. Rather, it corresponds to what recent philosophers have called a second naïveté. If dance is a language of the body and conceptual language that of the mind, tongues is the proper language of the spirit (see chapter 2, which discusses body, soul, and spirit). It is the heart talking to God beyond the limits of ordinary speech. St. Augustine called it "jubilation." In one of his commentaries on the psalms, the bishop of Hippo used the example of the North African practice of harvesters singing as they work. For a while, they sing traditional rhythmic songs to give cadence to their labor, but then "they discard the restricting syllables. They burst into a simple sound of joy, of jubilation. Such a cry of joy is a sound signifying that the heart is bringing forth what it cannot utter in words. Now, who is more worthy of such a cry of jubilation than God himself, whom all words fail to describe?" (*On Psalm 32*, Sermon 1, 7-8).

Cultures that are less verbal than ours understand this phenomenon very well. In our culture, we are so dependent on words that we are more afraid to do without them than Linus is to lose his security blanket. It takes the humility of Zacchaeus to let go of our self-image and surrender to what at first sight appears foolish. The tax collector was the richest man in town, and he probably defrauded some people to get to the top. That gave him a sense of importance. But he heard that Jesus was in town, and he went out on a limb to see him. An adult, in a moment of grace he became a child and climbed a tree. That act of humility brought Jesus to his house, launched him on a new life, and immortalized him as an example for all generations.

Some people don't yield to tongues, because they think that tongues means being miraculously zapped with a foreign language like Chinese or Tegalu or Swahili. Although the Pentecost story in Acts 2 might lead one to think that the disciples were all speaking foreign languages, the miracle was really one of *hearing*, something that Luke says three times (Acts 2:6, 8, 11). And Paul says that the interpretation of tongues comes as a gift in prayer, not in knowing languages (1 Corinthians 14:13). From my experience of composing songs, I can say that there is a parallel here with musical inspiration. Sometimes a melody comes first, the words later. When the words come after the melody, they fit the mood of the melody, and there can be more than one verse. Similarly, when one person speaks or sings in a tongue, another person in prayer, under the inspiration of the Spirit, picks up the mood and offers words that crystallize a meaning for the assembly. Another person may pick up the sense and offer a further interpretation, just as one might write a second verse to the same melody. The gift of tongues, then, is a prayer of the heart that bypasses words. All prayer, of course, should be prayer of the heart, but prayer in tongues has neither support nor restriction from words. It is just heart-to-heart prayer. It can, or course, dispose us to hear a "word of the Lord," either in the mind or via a Bible verse that we turn to.

Occasionally, by way of God's special providence, a word may be spoken in tongues that is recognized by another as a word of a known language. This once happened to me. A religious sister, a Native American of the Sioux nation, had just learned that her father on the reservation had been murdered. Grieving greatly, she asked me to pray with her, and I did so, partially in tongues. She later told me that one of the words I used was *waka*, which in the Sioux language means "Great Spirit." At the moment I said that word, she said she experienced the resurrection of her father. It was a great consolation to her, and although I had no idea of what I was saying in tongues, the Lord used it to convey his love and care for her at a very difficult moment.

The Gift of Praise

Can you receive the Holy Spirit without the gift of tongues? Of course. But Paul encouraged his readers to seek the gifts, even saying he wished they would all speak in tongues—which means that not everyone did (1 Corinthians 14:1, 5; 12:30). At least we can yield to the gift of praise, repeating short praise phrases like, "Glory to you, Lord Jesus," "Praise you, Father," "Bless you, Lamb of God," and so on.

Praise can change your day. There are mornings when I get up and feel like saying, "Good morning, God!" And there are mornings when I wake up and feel more like saying, "Good God, it's morning!" It was one of the latter mornings that I pulled myself out of bed and forced myself to drive to the airport to catch a flight to New Orleans, where I was to appear on a television program. How could I do that in the mood I was in? Then I remembered a line from Psalm 51: "I will offer a sacrifice of praise." "I don't feel like praising," I thought, "but maybe I can offer praise as my morning sacrifice." So I began praising the Lord. After all, he is not less worthy of praise just because I don't feel like praising him. A couple of songs and singing in tongues accompanied the hum of the Toyota I was driving, and by the time I reached the airport I didn't need a plane in order to fly!

Down in the dumps? Try offering the sacrifice of praise.

Another outlet of the Spirit is the gift of *prophecy*. To many, "prophecy" means predicting the future. It catches the eye on the tabloids at the grocery checkout. Jeane Dixon won a lot of attention with her "prophecies." People consult psychics and fortune-tellers to learn about their future. That's not what biblical prophecy is. Already in the Old Testament, the authentic prophets were those who proclaimed a *now* word from the Lord. A blessing or curse was promised, but the outcome was dependent on the choices, good or bad, that the people would make in the light of the covenant. As the written word in the Torah became more prominent, teachers of the law began to feel that sufficient revelation was made in the written word, and the voice of prophecy waned. But when John the Baptist began shouting his call for repentance in the desert, people called him a prophet, and so did Jesus (Matthew 11:9). He called people to conversion in view of the coming kingdom of God. They recognized in him the authentic voice of one like Elijah of old.

When the Holy Spirit came upon the community in the upper room, Peter said that the prophecy of Joel was being fulfilled, that "your sons and daughters will prophesy. . . . I will pour out a portion of my spirit on my servants and handmaids in those days, and they shall prophesy" (Joel 2:28; Acts 2:17-18). We can see from the event Luke describes that prophecy included the kind of ecstatic praise of tongues plus making "bold proclamations" (Acts 2:4; 4:31). The latter would refer to brief utterances inspired by the Spirit, as well as boldness in preaching. When Zechariah's tongue is loosed and he burst forth in a spontaneous hymn called the *Benedictus*, Luke said that he was prophesying under the power of the Holy Spirit (Luke 1:67-79). Thus prophecy could refer to an understandable, spontaneous praise flowing upward, as well as to an understandable, spontaneous message flowing outward to the assembly. Paul praised the gift of prophecy precisely because of its intelligibility and thus its potential for building up the community. Although he urged the Corinthians to seek the gifts, he especially urged them to seek the gift of prophecy (1 Corinthians 14:1-5).

So how do you seek the gift of prophecy, and how do you recognize it once it is given? The seeking is primarily praying for it, and the best kind of prayer is one that puts you in a listening mood. "Speak, Lord, for your servant is listening" (1 Samuel 3:9). If you have the gift of tongues, a period of praying with that gift will help dispose you to quiet within. A lake that is whipped into waves will hardly notice when a boulder is thrown into it. But if it is calm and still, a mere twig will send ripples a long distance. Don't be afraid to wait for the word. Waiting itself is prayer.

It will help to read something about the gift, such as one of Fr. Robert DeGrandis' little books.[8] And if you know someone who uses the gift, ask them how it works for them. Many prayerful people, I believe, have the gift but don't recognize it. When you pray, do you sometimes get an image, maybe even a vision (which is more common than we might think)? That is the seed of prophecy. The image may already be charged with meaning, but sometimes you need to ask the Lord or the Blessed Mother what the image means. Or a sentence or maybe even the beginning of a sentence may come to mind, and that could be the beginning of the prophetic gift. Sometimes you will open your Bible and a verse will jump out at you, as if spiritually flashing as a *now* word for you. The word may be thousands of years old, but it comes alive for you at this moment. All these are examples of how the Holy Spirit activates the word in us.

The next step is to ask whether what you are experiencing is just for you, or whether the Lord wants it for the entire group. If there is doubt, you might check it out with one of the leaders of the prayer group before sharing it publicly. If it seems appropriate for all, then cast aside any fear you might have and share it. It may be precisely what someone in the group needs to hear. And often that person will give testimony about how that word helped them. That is the power of prophecy. And in this way you can see how, by inspiring one person with a message for another, the Holy Spirit builds up the community in love.

The purpose of New Testament prophecy, Paul says, is "to build up, encourage, and console" (1 Corinthians 14:3). While this does not exclude challenge, the heart of the gift is to bring the hearer into a deeper union with Father, Son, and Holy Spirit, which only love can do.

So "seek earnestly the spiritual gifts, but especially that you may prophesy" (1 Corinthians 14:1). Sharing the word is thus another way of letting the living water flow through you, and in the process, keeping the Spirit alive within you and bringing refreshment to others.

....

Lord Jesus, I ask for your gifts of praise and prophecy, not to satisfy my pride but to glorify you more and more. Do in me what you did in Mary, making her a vessel of praise and a listening heart. Amen.

Chapter 18

Gifts, Part II

While working as a federal undercover agent, Frank Garcia was shot eight times during a drug bust. Miraculously he survived, but one of the shots had entered his right hand, leaving the last two fingers paralyzed. He had played the keyboard, and the injury severely limited his ability to play.

When Frank heard that the Voices of Victory, a Catholic singing group, was losing its keyboard player, he knew that he would be unable to replace the retiring artist, and that the group's ministry would likely have to end. The music group happened to be ministering with Fr. Robert DeGrandis in Clovis, New Mexico, during a healing service that Frank attended. At one point in the service, Fr. DeGrandis said that someone's hand was being healed. At that moment, a severe pain shot through Frank's hand and he began to move the paralyzed fingers. His hand was completely healed, and as of this writing, years later, he is still playing the keyboard for a singing ministry.

At a Mass during one of our Bible institutes at St. Mary's University, a woman received a "word of knowledge" similar to that of Fr. DeGrandis, except this time it was that someone was being healed of Parkinson's disease. I must admit that, standing at her side, I was skeptical, because I knew that medically there is no cure for Parkinson's. I had seen one of the participants, Nacho Gutierrez, coming into the Mass, his hands trembling as they had been for twelve years, forcing him to retire from his job and turn over the writing of checks to his wife. To my amazement, at the moment the word was spoken, Nacho's hands stopped trembling and he was able to use them normally. I have seen him often since, and while he may still have symptoms of the disease in his body, he always proudly waves his hands at me to show that they remain healed.

Recently, I was leading prayer for healing after Mass, and the woman who usually ministers with the word of knowledge, was not there. However, something told me that such a ministry was needed. I am still learning about the gift of the word of knowledge; it's still a mystery to me. But I felt that the Lord wanted it and that the people needed it. I was feeling a pain in my neck and shoulder, so I guessed that might be the place to start. "Someone is being healed of pain in their neck and shoulder," I began, and then added with hardly any reflection, "and someone is being healed of breast cancer." When I asked if there were any reports of healings in the congregation, two people said they were healed of pain in their neck and shoulders. Thank you, Lord. But there was no report of anyone's sensing a healing of breast cancer. Well, Lord, you and I are batting fifty percent, or maybe you're batting a hundred percent, and I, zero. Maybe the other word of knowledge was just my imagination. But the next morning I got a call from Christine, who told me that when she heard the word about healing of breast cancer, she felt a vibration in her breast. She had a lump the size of an egg that was so painful it kept her from sleeping well at night. But that night, she slept without pain for the first time. And the lump in her breast had disappeared.

Healing for Today

I have experienced the healing of many in my ministry, which I have not bothered to record, but the above examples will suffice to show that the "gifts of healing" of which Paul speaks (1 Corinthians 12:28) are still alive and well in the church today. I learned that this was true in the Charismatic Renewal. Even after my ordination to the priesthood, I thought that healings were very rare. They might happen through the sacrament of what we called "Extreme Unction" in those days, or through the intercession of some saints, or possibly at Lourdes. But I never really thought of myself as having the gift of healing. Yet I have seen so many people healed through prayer, my own and others', that I not only believe but know that Jesus continues what he began two thousand years ago: "Amen, amen, I tell you, whoever believes in me will do the works I do and will do even greater ones, because I am going to the Father" (John 14:12). "They will lay hands on the sick, and they will get well" (Mark 16:18).

Notice that this promise is not given to a select few. If you believe in Jesus, you have the power to heal. It is Jesus who heals, but he uses simple, sinful people like you and me today to do it. Most people don't realize that and consequently don't use the gift. It is true that some people have a nationally known ministry of healing. Praise the Lord for that. But it is possible that too much focus on extraordinary healers can lead Christians to forget that their baptism is their entitlement to the gift of ministering healing to others. St. Hilary, a doctor of the church, said around the year A.D. 350 that all the baptized receive the gifts of healing:

We who have been reborn through the sacrament of baptism experience intense joy when we feel within us the first stirrings of the Holy Spirit. We begin to have insight into the mysteries of faith, we are able to prophesy and to speak with wisdom. We become steadfast in hope and receive the gifts of healing.[9]

Even more important and more common than the remarkable physical healings like those mentioned above are the healing of emotional or spiritual illnesses. Our physical illnesses are like the part of the iceberg we can see. The larger part is beneath the surface, and in God's eyes that part is much more important. Most of us are scarred from memories of hurts, some of which may even go back to childhood. If we have suppressed those memories, they nevertheless affect our current behavior without our realizing it. I remember dealing with one young adult who was asking to apply to our community. In the course of our conversation, he said he could not remember anything that happened before he was ten years old. That shocked me, but it turned out that he had been severely abused during those years, and those memories were just too painful for him to think about. Nevertheless, his current behavior was affected by that trauma. Some people, however, don't suppress their hurts; they further irritate them. Perhaps someone has hurt me, and I keep aggravating the wound by constantly harping on it. If I'm not talking about it, I think about it, and I may even lash out at anyone who resembles the offender. My wound is a badge of honor, and at its worst it gives me the right to sabotage or at least hold back from the initiatives of others. The ultimate healing in both cases is forgiveness.

So why do some people get healed and others not? First of all, our God is not a slot machine. He is a person, and our personal relationship with him is what is most important. As St. Monica was praying over a period of seventeen years for the conversion of her son Augustine, she was growing in holiness, drawing ever closer to the Lord. Second, our priorities, which usually have to do with physical healing, are often not God's priorities. The inner spiritual and emotional wounds are usually what get his attention first. Third, there is one healing promised to every believer: the resurrection. Occasional healings of individuals are there to awaken the faith of the community by showing that if God can heal physically, he can also raise the dead to life. In this life, healings are signs to strengthen our faith in our ultimate destiny.

God Always Answers Our Prayers

For anyone who begins to pray with others for healing, it's important to keep that truth in mind, as well as the truth that God will answer our prayers in one way or another. In the early days of the Charismatic Renewal, I envied the healing gifts of Francis MacNutt, who has a nationally known healing ministry. Wondering what kind of faith or other dispositions he had when he prayed for healing, I asked him, "Do you know ahead of time that someone you are praying for is going to get healed?" It was a great relief to me when he replied, "No. All I know is that God is going to do *something*. It's up to him to answer as he pleases." Since then, I have been quite relaxed and confident in praying, because I have a new understanding of Jesus' promise, "Ask and you will receive. Seek and you will find. Knock and the door will be open to you. For whoever asks, receives; and the one who seeks, finds; and to the one who knocks, the door will be opened" (Luke 11:9-10). He did not say that we would get exactly what we asked for; but if not, we know that he is doing something because of our prayer, giving or preparing the person for something even better—and maybe what we asked for he will give eventually. Thus the person praying should not fear embarrassment if the prayer does not *seem* to be answered immediately. We know God is doing *something*.

The important thing is to *begin*. If you are a parent, lay your hand on your child and ask the Father or Jesus to heal your dear one. If the child is old enough to understand, ask them if you may pray for them. The faith, the desire, and the request of the one being prayed for are even more important than yours. And that holds true even more so when you are praying for adults. Ask permission, as well, if you wish to use touch, to lay your hand on the person's head or shoulder, or to hold their hands while praying. Respect the person's feelings at all times. Jesus even asked the beggar of Jericho, "What do you want me to do for you?" (Mark 10:51). To begin your prayer, it helps to recall a scene of Jesus healing someone, as well as his promise that if we ask, we will receive. The word of Jesus is powerful for building up the person's faith as well as your own. Perhaps before concluding your prayer, ask the person to join you in saying the Our Father. End by thanking the Lord for hearing your prayer, and give him the glory.

Healing was Jesus' favorite means of evangelization. It was his healings that drew the crowds and enabled him to have a huge audience for the Sermon on the Mount. Matthew tells us they came from Galilee, the Decapolis, Jerusalem, Judea, and beyond the Jordan (4:25). Why did Jesus begin that way? If you have a headache, it is very hard to listen to anybody. But if the speaker heals your headache, you will be eager to hear what he has to say. Jesus knew our body-soul makeup very well.

But there was another purpose to his healing ministry. In Matthew, the first healings Jesus did were all for marginalized people. The leper was quarantined from his village. He had to ring a little bell or a rattle when people approached and cry, "Unclean, unclean!" The centurion was a Gentile, for whom many Jews used the epithet "dog." And because she was a woman, Peter's mother-in-law was considered a second-class citizen whose witness was not allowed in court (Matthew 8:1-15). The sick in general were marginalized because many considered sickness a result of sin. Jesus' healings are implicitly a call for social justice and that love of neighbor that knows no boundaries. Through them, he tells us that God cares for everyone—even those that no one else seems to care for.

....

Lord Jesus, I ask that through prayer I may be able to minister your healing to others. Please give me that gift of the Holy Spirit. There are so many of my brothers and sisters who are suffering physically, emotionally, or spiritually. May I feel your love and compassion for them when I pray for them, that they may come to know you in the touch of your grace. Give me the faith to know that no prayer of mine goes unheeded. Give me healing hands and a healing heart, for your honor and glory. Amen.

Chapter 19

Gifts, Part III

The charisms of the Holy Spirit are not the same as our natural talents, although they can build on them. They are gifts that come to us out of the wellspring of God's love for the building up of the community in faith, hope, and love. In 1 Peter 4:10, they are divided into word gifts and service gifts: "As each one has received a gift, use it to serve each other as good stewards of the manifold grace of God. Whoever speaks should do it with the words God gives; whoever serves should do it with the strength God provides."

The Word Gifts

The word gifts include the word of knowledge, the word of wisdom, prophecy, interpretation of tongues, and discernment of spirits. We discussed prophecy and the interpretation of tongues in a previous chapter. The word of knowledge can be twofold. It may be the sharing of an insight into the faith, or it may be the knowledge of a fact that could not otherwise be known. When Jesus revealed to the Samaritan woman that she had had five husbands and that the man she was living with was not her husband, that was a word of knowledge (John 4:16-18). When Nathan told David of his sin (2 Samuel 12:1-12), if the prophet had not learned of it from any human source, that was a word of knowledge. Sometimes in prayer meetings you will hear a person call out that someone is being healed of a particular illness. If it proves to be true (I've seen healings happen like this), that is an authentic word of knowledge. It is one of those outlets for the Holy Spirit to witness that Jesus is risen and continues his healing ministry today. Like the other gifts, you must first pray fervently for it. Then you need to wait upon the Lord for the activation of this gift, which might happen in a prayer meeting, when you get a strong sense that a particular malady is being healed. It might come to you in the image of a particular organ of the body. Sometimes the gift might come as an inclination to call someone, and you discover that the person was in a crisis precisely at that moment.

The word of wisdom is an inspired counsel on how to live the Christian life. It can be given in a public setting or privately to a person seeking light for the path they should follow. On the personal level, however, beware of telling someone, "The Lord told me to tell you. . . ." This could be devastating to the person, especially if you have something negative to say, and besides, can you be sure that this was the Lord speaking and not your own ego? Rather, approach the person with a question, for example, "Do you find it difficult to. . . . ?" or "May I share with you a concern of mine?" Ask the Holy Spirit to give you the words, assuming that you already have discerned that you should say something to the person. Always get the person's permission before sharing your concern, and do so with the humility that you may be wrong.

The word of wisdom is closely related to the gift of discernment. Discernment is the light of the Holy Spirit identifying where there is evil. It is also the gift we need to choose the better path among various good options. This is the sense of Paul's prayer, "This is what I pray, that your love may abound more and more in knowledge and discernment, that you may judge well among the options before you" (literally, "among the things that differ") (Philippians 1:9-10). If, after searching out the pros and the cons of the various options, there is no clear preference that emerges, pray fervently and then choose either one. This is what the apostles did after the ascension of Jesus. They wished to replace Judas, so they prayed and two names surfaced. Unable to proceed further, they chose by lot, and Matthias was numbered among the twelve apostles (Acts 1:23-26).

The Service Gifts

There are other gifts too numerous to mention (celibacy and marriage are charisms in 1 Corinthians 7:7), but I would like to focus on the service gifts. What did Mary do as soon as the Holy Spirit came upon her? She hastened to serve Elizabeth, who was in her sixth month of pregnancy, even delaying her hymn of praise until she met her cousin. Mary was also alert to the needs of others at the wedding feast of Cana. And Jesus, endowed with all the charisms, said that the whole purpose of his coming was not to be served but to serve, even to the giving of his life (Mark 10:45). Of course, as we can see from the teaching of Jesus and from the few but key words of Mary, even the Spirit's word gifts are a service to the church. However, since 1 Peter 4:10 distinguishes service gifts from word gifts, I will do so here.

"Assistance" and "administration" are listed in 1 Corinthians 12:28). Paul does not elaborate further on what these gifts are. I think we can assume that the Holy Spirit's gift of assistance can be seen in those who offer to serve the community and do so in a cheerful, joyful, and committed way. And "administration" could refer to those who distribute the goods of the community to the poor, or to those who exercise leadership in the community.

But how do you tell the difference between those who are naturally disposed to these services and those who are exercising the charismatic service gifts of the Holy Spirit? The first letter of Peter gives the answer: "Do it with the strength God provides" (4:11). It is rather easy to see whether a person is doing a job or whether he or she is doing a ministry. Once when I ordered a book by telephone, I could not tell whether I was talking to a real person or to a machine, so lackluster was the voice of the lady on the other end. She must have been having a bad day. She gave me the impression that she really didn't want to talk to me at all. She certainly did not seem to be doing her job "with the strength that God provides." She needed prayer more than I needed a book. On the other hand, when I call Ann, a secretary in our provincial office, she gives me the impression that she's been waiting all year for that call. I look forward to the boost she will give me when I call. Hers is not a job; it's a ministry.

Enthusiasm, however, is not the only sign of the charism of service. When Peter speaks about doing our ministry with the strength that God provides, his words suggest that the gift proves itself in commitment and perseverance. There are people who are butterflies, hopping from one thing to the next. They don't hang on to anything very long. That's not how the gift of service works.

Music is certainly a gift. St. Augustine said that the two things on earth that are closest to heaven are music and the eyes of children. Some people have a natural gift for music, and when they develop it they can perform professionally. But it takes practice. Can music be a charismatic gift of the Holy Spirit? Yes, if it is a ministry, and if that ministry has the obvious anointing of the Holy Spirit. How do you tell? By the effect it has both on the choir and on the congregation. A musician may be very talented, but if he or she acts as king or queen of the choir loft, so wedded to the perfection of the performance that the other ministers are terrorized, that is hardly a gift of the Holy Spirit. On the other hand, if choir and congregation experience the music not as a performance but as an inspiration to worship, then the Holy Spirit is working through the ministry. Having had some experience as a musician myself, I know how difficult it is for some musicians to work with other musicians, because it takes adjustment and compromise. But with the Holy Spirit, everything is possible.

It is important for those who prize gifts like tongues, prophecy, and healing not to despise the service gifts. The smooth running of any community depends on them, and as Paul says, every member has an important ministerial role to fulfill. If you claim to be Spirit filled and are not willing to help with the chairs or clean up after fellowship, I would suggest that you pray for the gift of service. Thus, it would be helpful, I think, if those who are proficient in the word gifts would seek to balance their giftedness with service gifts, just as it would be helpful for those with service gifts to enrich their service with word gifts. But that doesn't mean you are called to be proficient in all the gifts. Rejoice with those who have gifts other than yours.

....

Lord Jesus, I want to be your servant, your instrument in bringing faith, hope, and love into the lives of others. For that I need the gifts of your Holy Spirit, the word gifts and the service gifts. Please show me what gifts I most need, and help me to grow in the ones you have already given me. Let me not think that my natural talents are sufficient to build your kingdom. Take what you have given me by nature and transform it by the anointing of your Holy Spirit. May I, like your mother, be moved to praise, to listen to your word, to share it, and to serve. Amen.

Body

What do you think of your body? Most of us would probably see it as a hindrance to our spiritual growth, especially since we have to struggle against a culture that is crazed either by indulgence of the body or excessive concern about looks. Indeed, there are religions that seek a complete escape from the body, as for example, Jainism, which is most widespread in India:

> Jainism . . . involves a separation and isolation from the body, a repulsive waste-ridden material object that represents entrapment in the cycle of rebirth. . . . One must cease identification with the body in order to realize the inherent godhood of the soul. Thus, the Jain ascetic seeks a mystical state whereby he realizes his true identity as pure soul. The ascetic sees the body in a negative light as that which binds him to the world as a result of karma. Accordingly, he should not enjoy his bodily experience. Rather he should strive to escape this bondage.[10]

Ritual death by starvation, though practiced by few, is the ideal death in Jainism.[11]

As Christians, we would certainly not agree with such a condemnation of what God from the very beginning pronounced as very good (Genesis 1:4-31). Indeed, God formed the human body from the earth (2:7), and humankind will forever live in solidarity with it, for we are *adam* from the *adamah*, earth man from earth. And the greatest scandal to religions like Jainism is that God should choose to take on a body, to be in complete solidarity with us, yes even in our bodiliness, and that the nailing of his body to the cross should be the price of our salvation. And even more, eternal life is not just immortality for the soul; it is resurrection of the body, Jesus' body first, then ours. As Catholics, we believe that Mary has been assumed bodily into the glory of heaven.

What has the Holy Spirit got to do with the body? Plenty. As we saw in chapter 2 ("But How Can This Be?"), each of us is spirit, soul, and body, a three-fold dimension of the human person; and our spirit, our openness to the beyond, to the transcendent, is our potentiality for union with the Holy Spirit. But our spirit is also intimately connected with our body; and the Holy Spirit, who is joined to our spirit, is not the enemy of the body, he is its friend. But just as friends don't let friends drink and drive, the Holy Spirit doesn't want our bodies to burn eternally in hell or take a single step that leads there.

Destined for Eternal Glory

The good news is that we don't have to, for in the Holy Spirit our bodies are destined for eternal glory. It all started with Jesus, whose body was formed in Mary's womb by the Holy Spirit and was raised from death by the same Holy Spirit (Romans 1:4). Jesus' glorified body is the source of the Holy Spirit. "'From within him rivers of living water will flow' . . . .

He said this of the Spirit that those who believed in him were to receive. For there was no Spirit yet, because Jesus had not yet been glorified" (John 7:38-39). He is the rock in the desert that gives an abundance of water to drink (1 Corinthians 10:4), the Lamb with God on the throne from whom the river of life-giving water flows (Revelation 22:1).

So how do we get connected with this glorious body that is the source of the Holy Spirit? By faith and baptism: "In one Spirit we were all baptized into one body, whether Jews or Greeks, whether slaves or free, and we were all given to drink of the one Spirit" (1 Corinthians 12:13). That "one body" is not the collectivity of the church, as in the way we might speak of all the students of a school as "the student body." The body Paul is speaking about is the one risen humanity of Jesus, to which we are sacramentally but very really attached and from whom we receive the Holy Spirit. This becomes clear when we look at 1 Corinthians 6:13-20: "The body is not for fornication but for the Lord," Paul begins, contrasting the union with the risen Christ with the physical union with the prostitute. And then he adds, "and the Lord is for the body" (verse 13). It is as if Jesus' whole purpose now in his risen state is to be the principle of the risen life for his members: "For God raised Christ from the dead, and he will also raise us up by his power" (verse 14). Power here is equivalent to the Holy Spirit, identified in many places with the power of God.

Then Paul goes on to show how realistically he thought of our union with Christ: "Don't you know that your bodies are members of Christ? Shall I then take the members of Christ and make them the members of a prostitute? God forbid!"

(1 Corinthians 6:15). Consorting with a prostitute would be adultery, according to Paul, for it would mean leaving the marital union with Christ for another. "Don't you know that whoever joins himself to a prostitute becomes one body with her? For it says, 'The two shall become one flesh.' But he who joins himself to the Lord becomes one spirit with him" (verses 16-17). The word translated "joins himself" is the same Greek word both for union with the prostitute and union with Christ. It suggests a "clinging." To become "one spirit" with Christ does not deny the physical union Paul has just mentioned above in saying that our bodies are members of Christ. Rather, becoming one spirit with Christ defines the effect of our bodily (real, though sacramental) union with the risen body of Christ. The effect of this union is that we become one spirit with him. We do not cease to be body, nor does Jesus. But this bodily union is the beginning of our transformation by the Holy Spirit that will ultimately climax in the resurrection. "If the Spirit of him who raised Jesus from the dead dwells in you, then he who raised Jesus from the dead will bring your mortal bodies to life through his Spirit dwelling within you" (Romans 8:11). Again, when Paul speaks in 1 Corinthians 15:44 of the "spiritual body," which is that of the risen Christ and our ultimate destiny, he is not talking about a ghost. He is simply saying that the body, far from being lost, is transformed into a glorious state, a process which is already at work in us (2 Corinthians 3:17-18).

Paul goes on in 1 Corinthians 6:19 to use a similar image of the body-spirit relationship: "Don't you know that your body is a temple of the Holy Spirit, whom you have from God, and you are not your own?" Jesus had spoken of his body as the new temple (John 2:21), but Paul clearly states, in light of the previous texts, that the individual Christian's body is also a temple of the Holy Spirit, because his or her body is joined to the risen body of Christ. Paul was probably not thinking of the pagan temples he knew so well in Asia Minor and Greece, but of the temple in Jerusalem, which was still standing at the time of his writing this letter, some twelve years before its destruction. The temple had been for him, as a Jew, the place of the Lord's dwelling in the midst of his people. How could he think of transferring that image to the body of the Christian? Because he knew that now God is totally present in the risen body of Jesus and that whoever is joined to Jesus shares in the divine *shekinah,* the cloud of glory that overshadows him. What the temple once was, now every Christian is!

In saying, "You are not your own; you have been bought at a price" (1 Corinthians 6:20), Paul is making a further statement about the temple of the Holy Spirit that is the Christian's body. Slaves were bought and sold in Paul's day, as they were in our country prior to the Civil War. I have in my files notes made by my great-grandfather about the slave trade in the United States. His family did not believe in slavery, but his mother so much admired a neighbor's slave that she gave my great-grandfather his middle name, Thomas, after the slave, and that name has come down to me as my middle name (that's what the "T" stands for). My great-grandfather's scribbled note reads, "A good Negro man was like a good mule and sold in the South according to his make, size, and stamina. They were worth from $1,200 to $2,000 according to their make and build, just as mules sell today." He went on to say that they could be rented out for $10 a month or $120 a year. I've taken this diversion about our country's experience of slavery to try to bring home the reality of the institution that existed in Paul's day and to point out that slavery still exists in several countries today.

Paul says that we have been bought. Sometimes in the ancient world, benefactors would buy a slave in order to set him free. We were slaves, and Jesus paid the price for our freedom. We were captives, and Christ paid our ransom. "It was for freedom that Christ set us free," Paul wrote to the Galatians (5:1). But there is more. Imagine a benefactor coming to a slave market and buying a young woman who has been a slave all her life, setting her free, and then taking her as his bride. That is what Christ has done for us. Freed from slavery to the world, sin, and the devil, we now belong to Christ; and our wedding to him makes us his own, enjoying his own freedom and his inheritance.

But what a price Christ paid! "You were bought *at a price*"—his own bloody passion and death. Were we really worth that much? It's not that we had done him a great favor, as if a slave had saved the benefactor's life. On the contrary, we had been responsible for his death! What made us worthy was not our love for him but his love for us. Paid in full by the blood of the Son of God, that's how much he loved us! Like the merchant who sold everything he had to buy the pearl of great price, God gave up the best he had, his only Son, that he might have us.

Bodily Life as Liturgy

All of this also shows how precious even our body is. "Therefore glorify God in your body," Paul concludes (1 Corinthians 6:20). If our bodies are temples of the Holy Spirit, if we belong to Christ as his members, or as a bride becomes one body with her husband, then our very bodily life is meant to be a liturgy. Everything we do in our body should radiate the glory of God. How might we go about doing that? In many ways. The most obvious is the use of our body in prayer. In the liturgy, we kneel, stand, bow, make the sign of the cross, raise our hands, and give voice to our thanks and praise. In our private prayer, we can do the same, perhaps even dancing or prostrating ourselves on the floor. But outside of prayer time, there are as many ways to glorify God as there are minutes in the day. Our work can glorify God. Our rest can glorify God. Eating, exercise, bathing, even our driving (ouch!)—all can glorify God. And yes, our smile. I've been told it takes fifty-eight muscles to frown and only fourteen to smile. It doesn't depend how young or handsome or beautiful we look. Blessed Mother Teresa of Calcutta had more wrinkles in her face than furrows in a field, but she radiated a youthfulness of spirit that electrified people. She was a beautiful embodiment of 2 Corinthians 4:16: "Although our outer self is wasting away, our inner self is being renewed day by day."

In our day, when the body, especially the female body, is being trashed by pornography and indecent exposure, this text of Paul is a call to witness to the body's holiness. A few years ago, a headline in our diocesan newspaper read, "Is that a naked woman in that pew?" Martha Brinkman, the editor, thus introduced her recent experience in church, when a woman a few pews in front of her indeed appeared to be wearing nothing, for all that Martha could see was a bare back and legs, the rest being blocked by the pew. That experience inspired her article pleading for more modesty in women's dress, especially in church.

Paul was dealing with people who were splitting spirit and body, as if it were sufficient to give the spirit to God and then the body to the prostitute. But those who believe that their bodies are espoused to Christ and that their bodies are temples of the Holy Spirit know differently. What we do in our bodies, so dignified by their union with Christ, is not an indifferent matter. It is a beginning of the resurrected life here and now.

....

Lord Jesus, I am awed by the dignity you have given to the human body, first by becoming man and then by raising your body from death and giving me a share in your own divine life. You have joined me to your risen body and filled me with your Holy Spirit. Give me the grace of constant awareness of this holy state, that I may indeed glorify God in my body. Amen.

Chapter 21

Church

T he Spirit and the bride say, 'Come!'" This invitation, on the closing page of the Bible (Revelation 22:17), joins the church and the Holy Spirit as one voice. There are several possible meanings to this text. It could be a cry for the Lord to return, but most likely it is a fragment of an early liturgy inviting the candidates to come forward to the baptismal waters, where they will drink of the one Spirit (1 Corinthians 12:13). At any rate, it is the Holy Spirit, speaking through the church, who calls them forward, and the writer of the Apocalypse could think of no better way to climax his book than by inviting everyone, whether already baptized or not, to drink deeply of the gift of the Spirit. But it is not just the prophet who invites; it is the entire church, beautifully depicted in this last book of the Bible as the bride of Christ. The bride longs for the return of the bridegroom, but in the meantime she longs to share the gift of the Spirit with her children. I invite you to explore with me this union of the church and the Spirit.

In the previous chapter on the body, we saw how Paul used the image of the temple for the individual Christian's body: "Don't you realize that your body is a temple of the Holy Spirit?" (1 Corinthians 6:19). But earlier in the same letter, he had used that image for the community itself. He was trying to bring the Corinthians out of their cliques and rivalries to a realization of their identity as a church. "Don't you realize that you are the temple of God and that the Spirit of God dwells in you? If anyone destroys the temple of God, God will destroy that person. For the temple of God is holy, and you are that temple" (3:16-17). The "you" here is plural, referring to the community to whom the letter was addressed.

Do you hear the seriousness of Paul's words? God will destroy anyone who destroys his temple, the community. The Holy Spirit is the spirit of unity and love. Sowing discord in the church is one of the most serious sins, and it could merit one's destruction either in this life or the next. Obviously, the Corinthians didn't realize how serious their infighting is ("Don't you realize?" Paul said). If the Holy Spirit is the bond of love in the Trinity, he can be no less a bond of love among those who belong to Jesus. Thus Paul, in the *Magna Carta* of the church that we call the Letter to the Ephesians, urged the community, "Be eager to maintain the unity of the Spirit in the bond of peace" because there is "one body, one Spirit" (4:3-4).

Because the Holy Spirit dwells in the church, the church is holy (1 Corinthians 3:17). Baptism and the word have made her clean (Ephesians 5:26-27), but Paul realized that there were imperfections in her membership, and this caused him great anxiety. Like a priest witnessing the engagement of a couple, Paul said he had betrothed the Corinthian community to Christ: "I am jealous of you with the jealousy of God, for I have betrothed you to one husband, Christ, to present you as a chaste virgin to him. But I fear lest, as the serpent in its cunning seduced Eve, your thoughts may be corrupted from a sincere and pure commitment to Christ" (2 Corinthians 11:2-3).

Bear with me a moment to say something about this translation. Some translators use the word "espoused" for "betrothed," suggesting that the marriage rite has been completed. But the word "to present you" is a future infinitive in the Greek (which we don't have in English). That means that Paul was thinking about presenting the bride at the last day, having all her purity for her one husband. The marriage would be fulfilled and consummated in heaven. Paul was thinking of the betrothal in Jewish terms, like the situation in which Mary was promised to Joseph before the marriage was finalized and consummated. For all practical purposes, Joseph and Mary were considered married, and infidelity was considered adultery. So here, the church is committed to Christ, and her infidelity would be considered adultery. That becomes clear from another text in which Paul said that, as by intercourse two become one flesh, so union with the prostitute is infidelity to Christ (1 Corinthians 6:13-20).

The Bond of Love

Now, what does this mean in practical terms for us? I remember concelebrating a wedding Mass at which the priest told the couple, "This is the second marriage for both of you." That came as a shock to everyone, because they knew that this was the couple's first marriage. The priest went on to explain that their first marriage had happened when they were baptized. They were espoused to Christ. And marriage, he went on to say, is the joining of husband and wife within that first marriage, of which they will thereafter be an icon, a reminder to the whole church of her marriage with Christ.

Where does the Holy Spirit fit into this picture? He is the bond of love between Christ and his bride. The more real and active the Holy Spirit is in our life, the stronger will be our bonding with our first love, Jesus. As the Spirit takes over more of our life, the earthly bonds we share become stronger, whether these be in marriage or family relations or with friends or co-workers. Even enemies become lovable, because the Holy Spirit teaches us how to love them, forgive them, and pray for them.

If the Holy Spirit is the bond of love between Christ and the church, how do we explain the infidelities and sins of so many of the church's members? It is simply because the church is not yet in that state of perfection that she will enjoy at the heavenly wedding. It is possible in this life to "sadden the Holy Spirit" (Ephesians 4:30). The purity with which we appeared at our baptism has been soiled by subsequent sins, and that is the fear Paul expresses in his second letter to the Corinthians. We just don't live up to our spousal commitment.

But Christ still loves his bride. The Holy Spirit is still there—not just in the spotless holiness of Mary and the heroic holiness of the saints and martyrs, but also in the prodigal sons and the Mary Magdalenes. They have graced the bride with repentance and that "second virginity" that is available through the mercy of God. The church in this world is a mix of saints and sinners, of weeds and wheat, of tilapia and garfish. Jesus reminded us of that reality in the parables in chapter 13 of Matthew. That is why we need to judge the church not by the sins of its members but by the means of grace it offers and the possibility of becoming a saint within it. And only God is the judge in the end.

I learned the importance of this truth a number of years ago. In my first year of teaching as a young Marianist brother, I had a class of high school freshmen who gave me a ride for my money and kept it up when I ran out of money. I lost all discipline, and that class later proved to be a challenge even for the seasoned teachers. I think everyone breathed a sigh of relief when they graduated. Probably many of us thought we might be visiting them in jail some day. But years later, I met Joe, who had been president of that freshman class. At the time Joe was a student there, the school had been small and "co-instructional," with the nuns teaching the girls on one side of the building and the brothers teaching the boys on the other. Despite our attempts to keep them apart, most of the boys and girls had paired off and married. However, Joe told me that at their twenty-fifth-year class reunion, out of thirty couples there had been only one divorce—an incredible statistic nowadays. And not only did they have successful careers, most were involved in some kind of ministry in their parishes. They had looked like weeds to me, but they turned out to be the finest wheat.

In our day, the church has suffered scandals that would have made St. Peter faint. I am referring to the large number of clergy whose sexual abuse of children has sent shock waves from Rome to Los Angeles. One would think that this tragedy would have led scores to abandon the Catholic Church. Not among those who are practicing Catholics, however, as surveys have shown. And at the height of the sexual scandal, the contributions to the Vatican by United States Catholics surpassed those of any other nation. These are people who love the church, who know the stories of Mary Magdalene and the Twelve who abandoned

Jesus to the cross. Peter, the chief disciple, denied Jesus and yet was made the rock on which the church was built. Indeed, the city of God on earth, the church, was built on this repentant sinner, on his faith and his love. The Spirit of the bride may be saddened, but never crushed. And in the midst of scandals, he continues to make saints. "Where sin abounded, grace has abounded all the more" (Romans 5:20).

The Holy Spirit also empowers the church for mission. When Jesus was about to ascend into heaven, his disciples asked him if he was going to establish the kingdom of God at that moment. Jesus replied, "It is not for you to know the times and seasons that God has set by his own authority. But you will receive power when the Holy Spirit comes upon you, and you will be my witnesses in Jerusalem, in Judea and Samaria, and to the ends of the earth" (Acts 1:7-8). That means that when we receive the Holy Spirit, we enter into the mission of Jesus, we enter into the mission of the church. Every one of us has a mission to proclaim the good news of Jesus Christ.

Witnessing is a primary way of evangelizing. Pope Paul VI said that the world is converted more by witnesses than by words:. "Modern man listens more willingly to witnesses than to teachers, and if he does listen to teachers, it is because they are witnesses."[12] When St. Ignatius as a soldier read the lives of the saints, he said to himself, "What these have done, why not I?" I have seen many persons converted at retreats when they heard the testimonies of other people whose encounters with Jesus had changed their lives. But witnessing is not the only way the Holy Spirit empowers the church. He also does it through charisms, those gifts of the Spirit that move Christians to ministry.

Because I am an ordained priest, it is taken for granted that I love the church. But love of this bride of Christ and mother of us all is part of the endowment of every Christian. In the measure that the Holy Spirit becomes more active in us, our love for the church will inevitably grow. We will see the Holy Spirit not just as a wonderful gift for ourselves but as something we want to share with everybody. It is thus that "the body builds itself up in love" (Ephesians 4:16).

....

Dear Jesus, grant me a double portion of your Holy Spirit, that I may become church in my heart, for the church is your bride. Through your Spirit, give me a deep love for her, a love born of your own that took you to the cross. Mother Mary, you who embody the church perfectly and are the goal to which the entire church journeys, inspire me with your love for this, your family. Amen.

Chapter 22

Desert

Matthew, Mark, and Luke all agree that after Jesus was baptized, the first thing the Holy Spirit did was to lead him into the desert. This may shock the reader, who might think that once empowered by the Spirit, Jesus should have begun immediately to announce the kingdom, heal people, and cast out demons. Not so. He first needed to deepen what he experienced at his baptism. What did it mean for his life that the heavens were opened? That the Holy Spirit descended upon him? That the Father declared him his Son, his beloved? What consequences followed from that experience? What did this all mean for his mission? We are speaking, of course, of his human understanding. We can only speculate. The only thing the gospels tell us is that in the desert he was tempted by the devil, and that that was even the Spirit's purpose in leading him there.

Note that the Holy Spirit continued to be with Jesus in the desert. There is a difference, a huge difference, between the desert without the Spirit and the desert with the Spirit. Without the Spirit, the desert can bring death. Hundreds of Mexicans have perished trying to cross the sixty miles of Sonoran desert from Nogales to Tucson. Trying to escape poverty, they fell into the desert's merciless jaws of heat and dehydration. So, too, many seeking to escape their own spiritual poverty have perished in the desert of drugs, alcohol, sex, fame, or fortune. Life without God is death in the making. But the desert's greatest menace, thirst and hunger, can also be its greatest gift if it leads the sinner to realize that his pursuits are indeed a death-dealing desert and, like the prodigal son, he decides to return home. Thus, without the Spirit, the desert can be either death or an awakening.

What is the desert like with the Spirit? Mark tells us that Jesus was with the wild beasts (1:13). We wish the evangelist had told us what he meant by that statement. Do the wild beasts signify the spiritual struggle he had there, the kind of metaphorical "struggle with wild beasts" that Paul says he experienced in Ephesus (1 Corinthians 15:32)? Or did Jesus meet real beasts, the kind the martyrs of Rome encountered in the Coliseum? If the latter, Jesus' struggle would have been an inspiration to them in their suffering.

Jesus' Battle in the Desert

But it is also possible that Mark meant that Jesus turned the violence of the desert into the peace of Eden. This was the kind of peace that Isaiah had prophesied that the Messiah would bring, when the wolf would be guest of the lamb (in this case the Lamb of God!), the leopard would lie down with the kid, the calf and the lion would forage together (11:6-9). We do know that the Holy Spirit is the Spirit of peace (Ephesians 4:3). But he also provides a sword, the sword of the Spirit that is the word of God (6:17). And a battle ensued. For Satan appeared with his usual craftiness. "If you are the Son of God," he began, recalling the voice of the Father at the baptism, "command that these stones become loaves of bread" (Matthew 4:3). Satan knew that a quality that is claimed must be tested to see if it is authentic.

He appealed to vanity by inviting Jesus to show off, and then to the great hunger Jesus must have felt in his body. If he yielded to the temptation, Jesus would not only be obeying Satan, but he would also be defining his future ministry, as if he had come to create an economic paradise. He would later multiply bread—not for his own sake, however, but for those who had first been filled with the word of God (Matthew 14:13-21; 15:32-39).

Jesus himself had other food, the food to do his Father's will (John 4:34). And he parried Satan's bid with the sword of the Spirit, the word from Deuteronomy 8:3: "One does not live by bread alone but by every word that comes from the mouth of God." That word comes straight out of Moses' mouth, when he recalled the time the people were tested in the desert: "He let you know the pangs of hunger and then fed you with manna, a food which neither you nor your fathers knew, in order to show you that not by bread alone does one live, but by every word that comes from the mouth of the LORD." At a retreat that I was preaching, we decided to spend one of the days fasting. For lunch we all came to the table bringing our Bibles, and the only food we consumed was the word of God. After sharing and commenting on our favorite passages, we left the table refreshed and strengthened, more convinced than ever that we can't live on bread alone without feasting on the word of God.

In this first of Jesus' temptations, we learn not only that Jesus succeeded where Israel in the desert failed, but also how we are to combat temptation: with the word of God. The first temptation is a temptation of the flesh. We shouldn't think that once we are baptized in the Spirit, we become immune to temptations of the flesh. But the Holy Spirit gives us power to overcome them, and since the sword of the Spirit is the word of God, we should arm ourselves constantly by a daily prayerful reading of the Scriptures.

The second temptation related by Matthew is of a different kind. Satan perceives that Jesus was a holy man. If he could not defeat the "Son of God" with the flesh, he would try to do so in the realm of the spirit. Jesus had quoted the Scriptures. "Well, I can too," Satan reasoned, and as he suggested that Jesus jump from the pinnacle of the temple, he cited the psalm, "He has given his angels a command about you, and they will bear you up on their hands lest you strike your foot against a stone" (Psalm 91:11-12; Matthew 4:6). As Shakespeare would later say, "The devil can quote Scripture to his purpose."[13] How important it is to interpret Scripture correctly! There are Christians today who take a verse out of context, ignoring the fact that there are other verses in the Bible that put that verse in proper perspective. So Jesus countered with another verse from Deuteronomy (6:16): "You shall not put the LORD your God to the test."

Jumping from the temple to a soft landing would have been within Jesus' power, of course, but he did not come to awe the crowds with magic. When we see a magician do a trick, what is the question that immediately comes to our mind? "How did you do that?" But Jesus' miracles would be of a different kind. They would not be sideshows. Simon Magus thought that was what the Holy Spirit was for, and that he could have it from Peter for a price, but he got a stinging rebuke instead (Acts 8:20-24). Jesus' ministry would be the compassion of God reaching out to the poor, the alienated, the marginalized, the sick, and the possessed. He brought healing, not entertainment. And his healings pointed the people to what was really important in their lives: the kingdom of God in their hearts and the needs of those who have been pushed aside by the elite and the powerful.

When we receive the Holy Spirit, we receive power. And as we yield to the Spirit's charisms, we can expect signs and wonders. But the ego can feed on anything, even on the most spiritual and the most dramatic of gifts. Hence, our motive for seeking the gifts (which Paul tells us we should do in 1 Corinthians 14:1) should not be our personal glory but only the glory of God and the building up of our brothers and sisters in faith.

The final testing of Jesus is the temptation of the shortcut. Satan showed Jesus "all the kingdoms the world and their splendor" (Matthew 4:10). These, Satan said, belong to him. Jesus did not deny that statement. He also knew that the Father had sent him to bring the kingdom of God to earth, to transform all those kingdoms into communities of justice, love, and peace. That is exactly what makes this temptation so appealing. He could have the world he has come to save in a flash: no suffering, no cross. But the price? Adore Satan. Take Satan as your god. Did Jesus at this moment feel the temptation of the millions who would seek power by turning to the devil, if not directly, then by the occult, through black magic, Ouija boards, tarot cards, fortune-telling, superstition, or voodoo? That is the temptation of the shortcut to spiritual power. Many indeed there would be who would fall for this temptation, with crippling and imprisoning results.

Jesus knew there would be a price to pay, but it would not be adoration of the devil. It would be the price of his own blood, if that was the Father's will. And so, with another stroke of the "sword of the Spirit," the word of God, he dismissed Satan:

"The Lord your God shall you worship, and him alone shall you serve" (Deuteronomy 6:13).

Similar lessons can be drawn from this temptation for those who seek to live the life of the Spirit. Don't argue or even dally with Satan. Swing the sword of the Spirit at once and be done with him. This is particularly critical if you are tempted to "just taste" a little of the occult or superstition or any of those other shortcuts to power, a web that is ultimately entrapping and deadly. There are those, of course, who are immune to this kind of temptation because they adore instead the god of reason and therefore exclude any connection with the realm of the spirit. Satan doesn't have to worry about them, because they have chosen to serve something other than God anyway.

If and when you receive the baptism in the Spirit, this reawakening or fanning into flame the grace of your baptism and confirmation, realize that the Spirit may sooner or later lead you into the desert. Often, however, the Lord knows that we need a time of honeymoon after that initial grace. And so, like the disciples in the upper room, we may have a period of "spiritual drunkenness." That certainly happened to me. I had been in a desert that had made me hunger and thirst for something better. On Christmas Eve 1970, when brothers and sisters laid their hands on me, I found Ein Gedi, an oasis in the desert. The desert became a garden, and I was on Mount Tabor. There was an unspeakable boost of spiritual energy that I can only explain as gift. But eventually, the Lord led me into the desert to do battle with my own demons. However painful this purification process has been, however, I know the difference between this desert and the earlier one—and it's that the Holy Spirit was there with me. The process is not over, nor will it be until the Lord calls me out of this world of gardens and deserts to the eternal Eden.

If you find yourself in a desert after receiving the baptism in the Holy Spirit, do not be surprised. That's exactly what the Spirit did to Jesus—he led him into the desert. Unlike Jesus, in us there is much to be purified. God doesn't wait until we are perfect to give us the Holy Spirit. He gives it lavishly to whoever asks in faith. And the Spirit comes with his power gifts: tongues, prophecy, healing, even miracles. But he also is the spirit of holiness, and in all of us there is much work, much purifying to do. Don't think all is lost when your feet feel the hot desert sand, your cheeks the burning sun, your stomach the pangs of hunger. The Holy Spirit is leading you where Jesus went, and there he will show you what demons you need to face. But fear not. The very same Spirit who led Jesus into the desert is leading you, and he will empower you with his word to stand as champion over the world's greatest enemy.

....

Holy Spirit, help me to understand that you may lead me through many landscapes, from mountains and valleys to gardens and deserts. Help me to surrender to whatever landscapes you may choose for me. I praise you for the Tabors and the Edens but also for the deserts. I know that when you lead me into the desert, you will speak to my heart (Hosea 2:16). Like the Israelite pilgrims of old, show me how I can go from strength to strength on the journey to the heavenly Jerusalem, even turning valleys into springs of living water (Psalm 84:6-8; John 4:14). Amen.

Chapter 23

Cross

From within him will flow rivers of living water" (John 7:38). This was Jesus' promise, delivered on the feast of Tabernacles, as water was being poured on the altar in a symbolic request for rain. It was from the altar of the cross, when Jesus' side was pierced, that water gushed forth (John 19:34). The water was a symbol of the Holy Spirit, "whom those who believed in him were to receive" (John 7:39). Jesus' blood also gushed out, to tell us of the price Jesus paid for that water, the Holy Spirit.

Only one time, on Easter Sunday, did Jesus lay his hands on the disciples' heads and say, "Receive the Holy Spirit" (John 20:22). But the gospel tells us that rivers of living water, the Holy Spirit, would flow not just once but forever. The rivers of living water would flow from the crucified Jesus, the rock, struck now not by Moses but by a Roman soldier. The same truth was conveyed symbolically at the moment of Jesus' death, which John describes thus: "He handed over the Spirit" (19:30). This phrase has a double meaning: Jesus breathed his last (spirit standing for breath), and Jesus gave the Spirit to the church. Jesus' last breath was not defeat. It was victory, the achievement of his life's purpose: to bestow on his bride the gift of the person of the Holy Spirit. "O Tree of Life," the church will sing, "that bore such wonderful fruit." The cross is the tree of life that will grow forever in the heavenly Eden, bearing fruit each month and offering healing to the nations (Revelation 22:2).

Jesus' own baptism in the Holy Spirit was prophetic of the fruitful cross. The Holy Spirit that hovered over the waters of the Jordan would not only anoint Jesus for his ministry of preaching and healing but would also empower him to offer his life in a loving surrender for our sake. The Spirit would lead him to embrace the cross. Difficult as this reality may be for us to accept—as it was for the first disciples—this is what Jesus said in Mark 10:32-45, when James and John asked him for the first seats in the kingdom. Jesus asked them, "Can you drink the cup that I am drinking or be baptized with the baptism with which I am baptized?" (verse 38). What did Jesus mean? He was referring to his coming passion, but he said that that *is* his baptism, an obvious allusion to the Jordan event. So Jesus' baptism in the Holy Spirit was his empowering to preach, heal, and embrace the cross with devotion and love, as he concluded, "For the Son of Man has not come to be served but to serve and to give his life for the ransom of many" (verse 45).

It would be a comfort to our flesh if Jesus had said, "I am suffering for you so that you won't have to suffer, and I will give you the Holy Spirit as a painkiller." Indeed, because of Jesus' cross, we won't have to suffer eternal punishment. But Jesus also said, "If anyone wants to come after me, he must deny himself and take up his cross and follow me" (Mark 8:34). So what difference does the Holy Spirit make if we still have to suffer?

Empowered to Carry Our Crosses

On the one hand, we should not take the words of Jesus as some do, as glorifying suffering, as immediate acceptance of illness without seeking healing through prayer. Jesus did not hesitate in Gethsemane to ask the Father to take the cross away from him. And his many responses to the requests of people for healing tell us that he is delighted when we seek his healing touch. In our day, we have seen thousands of miraculous healings through prayer and the charismatic gift of healing. God obviously wants us to pray for healing, to pray for the lifting of all our burdens. But then there is Jesus' surrender to the Father: "If this cup cannot pass unless I drink it, your will be done" (Matthew 26:42). The Holy Spirit empowered Jesus to accept the cross and to carry it without complaint.

So, too, with us. The Holy Spirit is power, but power that manifests itself through our human weakness and suffering. This was Paul's point to the Corinthians. He had prayed three times that the "thorn of the flesh" might leave him. But the Lord said, "My grace is sufficient for you, for power is made perfect in weakness." Paul then concluded, "Therefore I gladly boast of my weaknesses, that the power of Christ may rest upon me. So I delight in weaknesses, in insults, in tortures, persecutions and troubles. For when I am weak, then I am strong" (2 Corinthians 12:9-10).

This is the Christian paradox: acceptance, even joy in suffering, not because suffering is good in itself or painless but because, after prayer for the release of it, the Christian accepts it as part of his or her vocation in following the Lamb. In this light, there is no wasted pain. It is the Holy Spirit that empowers our suffering to participate in the redemptive suffering of Christ, or as Paul said, "I rejoice in my sufferings for your sake, and I fill up in my flesh what is lacking in the sufferings of Christ for his body, which is the church" (Colossians 1:24). Christ's sufferings were of infinite value, but he chose to leave a little for us to do, that we might know his joy in suffering for others.

Most of our sufferings are of the kind that Paul speaks about in 1 Corinthians 10:13: "No trial has come upon you but what every human experiences. God is faithful. He will not let you be tested beyond your strength, but he will provide a way out that you may be able to bear it." But much of the suffering that our brothers and sisters experienced for the first two centuries was precisely because they *were* Christians. It was the age of the martyrs, who sowed with their blood, as Tertullian said, the great harvest of Christians that followed. ("The blood of martyrs is the seed of Christians.") Many of the martyrs expressed their joy at the honor of suffering with Jesus. Felicity was one of two women thrown to the beasts in the Roman arena. She was pregnant and gave birth to her child while in prison. The guard mocked her in her birthing pains, saying that it would be a lot worse when the beasts attacked her in the arena. Felicity replied, "My sufferings here are mine. But there another will be suffering with me." Every age of the church has had its martyrs, and more Christians have shed their blood in the last century than all other centuries combined. Jesus said that the Holy Spirit would empower his disciples to be witnesses (the original meaning of "martyr"). If, then, the Holy Spirit is the power that enables Christians to follow Jesus to a martyr's death, what power he must give us to carry our daily crosses!

Empowered to Overcome the Flesh

The cross, however, means more than acceptance of suffering. In Paul's mind it also empowers us to overcome the flesh, that tendency toward self-indulgence and pride that bedevils us even after we have become Christians. The cross is a teammate of the Holy Spirit to bring us to holiness. Paul was at pains to show the Galatians that Christ had freed them from the old law, but that freedom was not to be interpreted as license for the flesh. After listing the fifteen "works of the flesh," from immorality to "orgies and the like," he then said, "But the fruit of the Spirit is love, joy, peace, generosity, kindness, goodness, faith, humility, self-control." And then, framing the fruits of the Spirit with another reference to the vices, Paul wrote, "Those who belong to Christ have crucified their flesh with its passions and desires. If we live by the Spirit, let us walk by the Spirit" (5:19-25).

Notice how Paul alludes to the cross of Jesus by saying that Christians have "*crucified* their flesh." If the cross is the power of God and the wisdom of God (1 Corinthians 1:24), one of its effects in us is to nail our selfishness to the cross. That could be frightening to anyone who has not tasted the gift of the Holy Spirit. But to taste the Holy Spirit is to know love, for "the love of God has been poured into our hearts by the Holy Spirit who has been given to us" (Romans 5:5). When you know you are loved, you can let go of all those things you try to do to convince yourself that you are loved: stuffing yourself with food, hungering for praise and applause, or addictions of any kind. When you are filled with love, joy, peace, and the other fruits of the Spirit, you don't have to try to fill your emptiness with lesser things. And yes, one of the fruits of the Spirit is self-control. But all of this comes not from beating ourselves up but from letting God love us!

....

Lord Jesus, I make the sign of the cross frequently and so often routinely that I forget its meaning. It is one sign that proclaims God's love for a broken, sinful world, a love that led you to your death. What power that love gave to you! It was indeed the Holy Spirit who gave you that incredible energy. When you allow me to experience crosses, may they not be wasted. Empower me with the same Holy Spirit, so that I may consider it an honor to fill up in my flesh what is lacking in your sufferings for your body, the church. Amen.

Chapter 24

Word

Try speaking a word, any word. Notice the mechanics of your body when you do so. You have to breathe out, at least slightly. It's not impossible to breathe in while speaking, but it does feel weird. Word needs breath. God's Word needs the Spirit.

Within the holy Trinity, when God utters the Word, who is the second person of the Trinity, he also conveys to him the Holy Spirit. In this way, the Word, too, becomes a "breather" of the Holy Spirit. That's the way the theologians describe the Holy Spirit proceeding from the Father and the Son. They call it *spiration*, which is from the Latin word for "breathing." (In English "inspiration" means breathing in; "expiration" means breathing out.)

It was a long way from Genesis to this understanding of the Word and the Holy Spirit in the Trinity. But from our New Testament perspective, we can see a foreshadowing in the first creation story, where God's spirit prepared for his word. The spirit of God hovered over the waters, and then God spoke. The psalmist confirmed the image of Genesis by saying, "By the *word* of the LORD the heavens were made, by the *breath* of his mouth all their host" (Psalm 33:6).

Creation, all of it, from the farthest star to the tiniest flower, is a work of God's spirit and his word. So when we look at the beauties of nature, the clouds by day or the moon and the stars by night, if we are listening, they speak to us, they are a word of God to us, and they also tell us something about the creative Spirit of God. "The spirit of the LORD fills the whole world, and the universe acknowledges his voice (Wisdom 1:7).[14] As our breath empowers us to speak, and our words shape our breath into intelligible sound, so creation manifests the power of God, and his word gives it shape, consistency, order, intelligibility, and beauty. Not that we could come to know the inner mystery of the Trinity by contemplating nature. That mystery we know only because God in his great love for us chose to reveal it in Jesus Christ and the Holy Spirit: "Eye has not seen, ear has not heard, nor has it ever entered into the human heart what God has prepared for those who love him. But God has revealed these things to us through the Spirit" (1 Corinthians 2:9-10). But in creation, God left his fingerprints on every star and flower. And in the human person, he placed the highest resemblance so that, once revealed, the holy Trinity could be understood by analogy with the simplest human actions: breathing and speaking.

God's "Now" Word for His People

In the Book of Judges, the spirit of the LORD often moves individuals to perform heroic actions or to take up roles of military leadership: Othniel (3:10), Jephthah (11:29), Gideon (6:34), and Samson (13:25; 14:6, 19). At times, too, the spirit puts individuals or groups in a prophetic state, that is, a kind of ecstatic state that defies rationality (Numbers 11:24-30; 1 Samuel 10:10). But most of all, the spirit is attached to prophecy, the gift given to outstanding persons in the Old Testament, such as Hosea, who is called "the man of the spirit" (9:7). Micah says he is filled with power and the spirit of the Lord to declare to the people their sins (3:5-8).

This text is significant, because it tells us that the prophet is not someone who does extraordinary deeds like making military conquests, as in the Book of Judges, or even one who forecasts the future, but one who, by the spirit, speaks God's *now* word to the people, calling them back to the covenant. The prophets are the moral leaders of the people. They even shy away from too much emphasis on the spirit because the false prophets also appeal to the spirit, and so arises the need for discernment. Deuteronomy gives two rules for discernment: Is the prophecy fulfilled (18:21-22)? And does it concord with orthodox Yahwistic faith (13:2-6)? Paul will insist on the latter norm for discernment when he says that authentic prophecy must proclaim Jesus as Lord (1 Corinthians 12:3). Thus, prophecy can be discerned more easily than other non-rational movements of the Spirit, because it can be measured against God's truth already revealed in Jesus.

In the New Testament, the supreme icon or prototype of the relation of the Holy Spirit to the Word of God appears when the Incarnate Word is conceived in Mary's womb by the power of the Holy Spirit (Luke 1:26-38). As in eternity the Father generates the Son and gives to him a share in breathing forth of the Holy Spirit, so in time the Father begets his Son through the Holy Spirit in the womb of Mary. In effecting this miracle, the Holy Spirit, who is the mutual love of Father and Son, begins to pull aside the veil of the inner life of God.

More of the curtain was pulled aside when Jesus was baptized in the Jordan, where the Spirit descended in an outward form, and the Father's voice was heard. Jesus would speak and act in the power of the Holy Spirit throughout his ministry. He would cast out demons by the Holy Spirit (Matthew 12:28), and his words would be God's words, because the Father does not ration the Spirit he gives to Jesus (John 3:34). Finally, Jesus, himself the Word, gave the Holy Spirit to his disciples (John 19:30; 20:22).

This relation of the Word to the Holy Spirit emerges frequently in the Acts of the Apostles. No sooner had Peter received the Holy Spirit than he went out and proclaimed the Word to the people (Acts 2:14-41). "Filled with the Holy Spirit," Peter proclaimed his defense before the Sanhedrin (4:8), as did Stephen, the first martyr (7:55). Faced with persecution, the early community prayed, a second Pentecost occurred, the room shook, and all were filled with the Holy Spirit and continued to proclaim the word with boldness (4:31). While Peter was preaching to the household of Cornelius, the Holy Spirit fell upon the listeners, and they began speaking in tongues and glorifying God (10:46).

Similar experiences happened to me on two occasions while I was preaching, except that they were healings. At a retreat at Biscayne College in Miami, a man named Gus was healed of deafness during my homily at the closing Mass. In El Paso, Texas, Luz Escobedo's feet were healed while I was giving my personal testimony, and when I returned ten years later, she told me that her feet were still healed.

Is it any wonder that brothers and sisters who are prayed over for the baptism of the Holy Spirit often receive such a hunger for the word of God that they spend hours devouring the Scriptures?

They have indeed found that human beings cannot live by bread alone but by every word that comes from the mouth of God.

Enfleshing the Word in Our Lives

The most powerful wedding of the Holy Spirit and the word happens when Christians enflesh the word in their own lives. The saints are the word made flesh. An incident with my mother made that very clear to me.

I had been stationed in San Antonio for the previous twelve years, so I was able to visit my parents often—my father for the three years before he died, and my mother for the remaining nine years. Then, on Good Friday 1972, I received a call from my provincial asking me to take the position of rector of our seminary in St. Louis. This news, I knew, would come as a blow to my widowed mother, so I determined that she would be one of the first ones to hear it. I drove to the ranch, and after the usual initial pleasantries, I said, "Mama, I have to tell you something."

Sensing the seriousness in my voice, she left the pot of potatoes she was tending on the stove and said, "Well, let's sit down."

We did, side by side on the couch. "I'm being assigned to St. Louis," I began, "and that means I won't be able to see you very often." (Little did I know she had only two more years to live.)

She was silent for a while. Then a big tear rolled down her left cheek, and she looked at me and said, "Well, when you put your hand to the plow, it won't do to look back."

She was quoting the words of Jesus in Luke 9:62. As a biblical scholar, I can tell you that these words come neither from the Gospel of Mark, which Luke had before him, nor from the

"Q" source, but from Luke's special source, which the scholars call "L." But never had the meaning of that verse struck home to me as it did that afternoon, when my mother reminded me that if I was holding the plow in the straight furrow, so was she. The word became flesh again at that moment.

That is what all of us are called to be: the word made flesh. And whenever that happens, it is always by the power of the Holy Spirit, who worked the first and iconic enfleshing of the Word in the womb of Mary.

But just because we have received the Holy Spirit and exercise the Spirit's gifts, that doesn't mean that we automatically enflesh the word. Jesus warned us that just saying "Lord, Lord" is not sufficient to get us into the kingdom. Nor is it sufficient even if we have prophesied in his name, driven out demons in his name, and worked mighty deeds in his name. Those who do those things without living as Jesus tells us to live risk hearing his words, "I never knew you. Get out of my sight, you workers of iniquity" (Matthew 7:21-23). Paul made the same point when, in discussing the charisms in 1 Corinthians 12–14, he placed the chapter on love (13) in the center, for even the charisms are given for the sole purpose of building up the community in love. And that is why the next chapter in this book will be about the holiness that the Holy Spirit wishes to give us, which can be summed up in one word: love.

....

Lord Jesus, Word of God, conceived and enfleshed by the Holy Spirit, may your gift of the Spirit make me fall in love with your word. Let me be like Ezekiel and the author of the Book of Revelation, who ate the scroll of your word (Ezekiel 2:8-9; Revelation 10:9-10). Show me that I cannot live by bread alone but by every word that comes from the mouth of God. Mary, you to whom the Holy Spirit presented the Word of God as your son, intercede for this grace for me, and teach me how to receive the Holy Spirit so as to enflesh the word in my life. Amen.

Chapter 25

Love

In the days when movies were still in black and white, one that became an instant hit was *Marty*. Marty was a butcher in his thirties who was still unmarried because he had spent his time and energy taking care of his widowed and ailing mother. But Marty's buddies thought it was time for him to marry, so they arranged a meeting with a beautiful girl. Marty fell in love with the girl, but it took some time before he could overcome his shyness enough to tell her so. Yet tell her he did. One night, at the door of her apartment, he asked her to marry him. She acquiesced joyfully, and as he left her that night, Marty ran down the street singing and, with his big butcher's fist, knocked an octagonal stop sign and set it spinning.

That scene has stayed with me over the years, because it shows what can happen to people when they realize that they are loved. Marty was energized. He ran. He sang. And now no stop sign could stop him. That's what God wants us to feel when we know that he loves us. And the Holy Spirit is that "yes," that kiss, that embrace of the Father that tells us that he loves us. "The love of God is poured into our hearts by the Holy Spirit, who has been given to us" (Romans 5:5).

The good news is that he shows us his love even when we are sinners. One evening when I was ten years old, my father, my Aunt Margaret, and I stood for grace before sitting down to supper (my mother was not there, for some reason). As we prepared to sit, it occurred to me to be a gentleman and pull the chair away from the table and offer Aunt Margaret her seat. I swung around to her side of the table, pulled out the chair, and in the split second before putting it back under her, a little devil alighted on my left shoulder and said to me, "Wouldn't it be fun to see what would happen if you didn't put the chair back?" My guardian angel popped up on my right shoulder and engaged the little devil in a tug of war—but the devil won. I did reach down and catch my aunt before she hit the floor, but in another split second, I felt the sting of my father's hand with a powerful slap on my left cheek. Aunt Margaret, who loved me with an unconditional positive regard, came to my defense and said, "Oh, he was only trying to be helpful!" My father's grunt response was impossible to interpret.

The supper was unusually quiet. I toyed with my food, hoping we would finish rapidly so that I could escape to my bedroom upstairs. But that was no escape. Shortly I heard the heavy boots of my father mounting the stairs. And yes, he stepped on that one stair that always creaked as if in pain. It spoke for my anguish and fear. When my father's gargantuan frame filled the doorway, I froze. But the huge frame collapsed to its knees beside my bed, and he said, "George, I'm sorry I slapped you. Please forgive me." What could I say? That I really meant to do it? The only words that came to my mouth were, "That's okay." Then my father leaned over and kissed me on the forehead. I melted into the bed, speechless. I was punished and healed by love.

Punished by Love

I really believe that's what purgatory is all about. The only reason why we may not get into heaven immediately at the moment of our deaths is that we haven't received all of God's love for us. If we had, then we would be holy and purified and, if you will, punished. But punished by love, the way my father's love was punishing me. I felt more remorse because of that kiss than if he had given me a beating. That's the way Jesus healed Peter when he asked him, "Do you love me?" (John 21:16). That meant, "Are you willing to let me love you? Are you willing now, after your denial, to let me wash your feet as I did at the Last Supper? Just accept my love by saying that you love me, and that is all you need to do. Let me wash you now with love, and you will be clean."

That's the way God's love comes to us sinners. He first shows us his love outwardly: "God so loved the world that he gave his only Son, that whoever believes in him might not perish but might have eternal life" (John 3:16). Paul realized that Jesus shared the Father's love that took him to the cross: "He loved me and gave himself up for me" (Galatians 2:20). As I mentioned in an earlier chapter, that revelation of God's love in the historical act of Jesus' death on the cross becomes an interior experience when the Holy Spirit is given to us, and that is the gift of God's love: "The love of God is poured into our hearts by the Holy Spirit, who has been given to us" (Romans 5:5).

Once when I was praying before the Blessed Sacrament, I felt a very strong love for the Lord welling up in my heart. I asked the Lord, "Is what I'm feeling my love for you or your love for me?" And it seemed to me that the Lord's response was, "It's the same love." Indeed it is love, *agape*, God's love that he has poured into our hearts through the Holy Spirit, that links us even now to heaven. Faith will give way to vision, but the love in which we live now is no different than the love in which we will live in heaven. As Jesus said to me, "It's the same love." And that is because of the Holy Spirit.

The passage from Romans 5:5, which I have quoted twice, is at the conclusion of a section dealing with hope. Christian hope, Paul says, does not disappoint, because the love of God is poured into our hearts by the Holy Spirit. What he is saying is that the basis of our hope for eternal life is not just the promise God has made to every believer (John 3:16), but the fact that already now we have the Holy Spirit, the love of God in person, and the Trinitarian life that will be our everlasting joy in heaven is already begun in us.

The Holy Spirit is like a sunflower. The petals are all the gifts of the Holy Spirit, but the heart of the flower is love. If you pluck a petal and expect it to last, you will be disappointed when it withers in your hand, and so will anyone with whom you want to share it. The gifts of the Spirit are beautiful and alive when they are attached to love. Such is the message of Paul in chapter 13 of 1 Corinthians, the *Magna Carta* of love that is sandwiched between two chapters on the charismatic gifts. Paul did not even consider love a charism, for charisms can come and go, and not everyone has every charism. But love is a "way." It is a path that all are to travel because it is the path of Jesus. And he wants those who use the charisms (which he encourages) to do so in love.

Thus, more important than any of the gifts of the Spirit is the Gift of the Spirit. If, when you seek to be baptized in the Holy Spirit as a renewal of your baptismal grace, you experience the love of God at a deeper level, your prayer has been answered. And if your experience has been authentic, you will automatically feel the impulse to express that love in some way, and that is what the charisms are for.

The Holy Spirit is like a sunflower in another way. The petals are the members of the church, held together by the heart of the church, which is love. Thus, St. Ignatius, the bishop of Antioch, in his letter to the Christians in Rome on his way to being martyred there, addressed them as the community "pre-eminent in love."[15] If we don't understand the Holy Spirit as love, we have not understood him at all, and we have certainly not understood anything about the Trinity, for the Holy Spirit is the mutual love of the Father and the Son. And on earth, the church is not just the pope and the bishops and the buildings and Sunday Mass and all those other visible elements we think of as "church." The heartbeat of the church is the Holy Spirit, the throbbing of love in the Trinity that becomes the throbbing of love in the bride of Christ.

Because of this truth, the deeper we go into the treasure of the Spirit, the more we will fall in love with the church. However, the more, too, we will feel the pain at the fragmentation of the church among all those who claim Jesus as Lord. And the more we will be led to pray and work for its unity: "That they may all be one, as you, Father, are in me and I in You, that they may be in us" (John 17:21).

....

Lord, your saint, Thérèse, the Little Flower of Jesus, said she wanted to "be love." She wanted to be the heart of the church. She wanted to be what the Holy Spirit is, and no wonder, because the more we love, the more we become like the Holy Spirit, who is love. Lord, let me be love. Amen.

Chapter 26

Mission

When I was a student in Central Catholic High School in San Antonio, there was an annual mission drive. We would sacrifice some of our candy or movie money, or the change we had wheedled out of our parents, to support the foreign missions. Enthusiasm was whipped up by competition among the homerooms, many of which recorded their daily accrual on a huge thermometer. Missionaries were men or women who worked in far-off lands and inspired us by an occasional talk when they passed through town. Or, growing up in a town known for the Alamo and four other missions, we knew about the Franciscans and Dominicans and Jesuits who came from abroad to bring the faith to this country. Hence in my teenage years there was always something foreign and exotic about the notion of mission and missionaries. And later on, I would become one myself, spending six years in Nepal and India.

This missionary image is also what we have of the New Testament church as it spread rapidly throughout the Mediterranean and even beyond. Jesus told his disciples, "You will be my witnesses in Jerusalem, in Judea and Samaria, and even to the ends of the earth" (Acts 1:8). And that is exactly what happened. We know that this mission was not confined to the Twelve, although Luke certainly insisted that it should be in communion with them. Philip, not one of the twelve apostles, was the first to evangelize Samaria. Though in communion with the

Twelve, Paul independently evangelizes Asia Minor and what is today Greece and perhaps even parts of Spain. We do not know how the gospel first reached Rome. There was brisk commerce between Palestine and the capital of the Empire, so it is possible that lay business men or women were in Rome before any of the apostles. They would have shared their newfound faith with other Jews there. This "big-bang" model of the early church is the impression we get from the gospels.

St. Luke brings another dimension to the picture of the Spirit-filled mission. We find it in the first two chapters of his gospel, which provide a preface not only to the public life of Jesus but also to the Acts of the Apostles. Much of what happens in the infancy of Jesus is a forecast of what will happen in the infancy of the church in Acts. The Holy Spirit comes upon Mary, as he will come upon the church, making her interiorly fruitful and then sending her on a mission to the hill country of Judea, where she will share the good news with her cousin Elizabeth and help her through the birth of John the Baptist. Mary experiences a domestic Pentecost. And in their own way, so do Elizabeth, Zechariah, and Simeon and Anna, the prophetess. That is no less the work of the Holy Spirit than the collective explosion that occurred in the upper room after the ascension of Jesus.

Missionaries Where We Are

There is an important lesson here: what happens in the nest is just as important as what happens when the fledgling makes its maiden flight. There is a missionary activity that goes on in the home that is as important as the one on the road. Some in the church will be called to missions abroad. But all of us are called to be missionaries *where we are.* The Holy Spirit is given to be given, wherever we are. "Where can I escape from your spirit? From your presence where can I flee? If I climb to the heavens, you are there; if I sink to the nether world, you are there. If I fly with the wings of the dawn, if I land at the farthest limits of the sea, even there your hand will guide me, your right hand hold me fast. If I say, 'Darkness shall surely hide me, my only light will be the night,' for you darkness is not dark at all, and night shines like the day" (Psalm 139:7-12). There is no use trying to be a missionary outside if I am not a missionary at home. How to exercise that mission, of course, takes a gift of discernment (which is also a gift of the Holy Spirit). But just as Mary's first mission was to her own, so is ours.

The problem that many of us face, however, is that often those closest to us are the hardest to reach. Jesus himself was not well received in his own hometown. Perhaps the Lord allows these challenges in our lives in order to keep us on our knees. In those cases, having done what we could, we become missionaries through prayer. Such was the vocation of St. Thérèse, the Little Flower, who embraced hardened sinners and the farthest missions in her prayers. And sometimes outsiders may touch our family members more readily than we can. That can increase our humility, but also our thanksgiving. For, as Paul says, "What does it matter as long as . . . Christ is being proclaimed? And in that I rejoice" (Philippians 1:18).

The point is that to receive the Holy Spirit is to be launched on mission. So it was with Jesus, who was anointed by the Holy Spirit in the Jordan for his mission of preaching and sacrifice. So it was with the disciples in the upper room at Pentecost. So it is with us when the grace of our own baptism is released powerfully in the baptism of the Holy Spirit. Lack of response should not discourage us. "What God asks is not our success but our cooperation," said Marianist founder Blessed Fr. William Joseph Chaminade. Or, as Blessed Mother Teresa of Calcutta put it similarly, "Fidelity, not success." Like all water, the living water of the Holy Spirit moves first to the lowest level, where there is receptivity, and with time the water will rise to cover those lands higher up. God follows his timetable, not ours.

Team Spirit

But beware of "Lone Ranger" missions. Even St. Paul was not a Lone Ranger. He traveled and worked in teams. Notice how often his letters begin, "Paul and Sosthenes," or "Paul and Timothy," or "Paul and Silvanus and Timothy," or with similar addresses. If our mission comes from the Holy Spirit, it cannot be a fringe activity, for the Holy Spirit is the bond of unity, especially in mission. Sometimes the Holy Spirit may inspire us to a personal mission. But it will always be in communion with the bride, the church. The most successful missions are those we carry out with others, and that takes a great deal of communal asceticism or, if you will, team spirit. The San Antonio Spurs won four world basketball championships in ten years, and the secret was not just having star players. They worked together as a team, knowing that team victory was more important than personal glory. If you are in charge of a group with a mission, don't try to do everything yourself. Discover, encourage, call forth, and integrate the gifts of others. That was Paul's program for the growth of the church. In Ephesians 4:7-16, he says that each member of the church has received a gift. And then he points to some of the leadership roles in the church: apostles, prophets, evangelists, pastors, and teachers. But what is their role? It is to organize and bring together the *faithful* to fulfill *their* role in building up the body of Christ: "In order to mobilize the saints for the work of ministry for building up the body of Christ" (4:12).

The centrifugal model is not the only model of evangelization, however. In dealing with the charisms in the Corinthian community, Paul indicates that another method was very effective in the early church: attraction. He speaks about unbelievers or uninstructed persons who, coming into the community and being converted by what they experienced there, would fall down and say, "God is truly in your midst" (1 Corinthians 14:24-25). So the most effective means to evangelize someone might be to invite them to a prayer meeting. Many a conversion has happened that way.

All the faithful are called in some measure to build up the church. But the primary call of the laity is to transform the temporal order, to work toward bringing the kingdom of God into the workplace, into the world of politics, to work toward an economy that is just and mindful of the less fortunate, to transform the culture of death into the culture of life. That, too, is a work of the Holy Spirit. In one of the early liturgies of the church, reflected in two late manuscripts, "Thy kingdom come" in Luke's version of the Lord's Prayer is replaced by "Thy Holy Spirit come upon us and cleanse us." That suggests that the church understood that the coming of the kingdom is the work of the Holy Spirit. And that is why no Christian worthy of the name can be lethargic. The Holy Spirit must flow through us to build the church and God's kingdom in this world.

....

Lord Jesus, you are the missionary of the Father. You were anointed by the Holy Spirit to fulfill your mission, and you continue to send your Holy Spirit upon your church, just as you did at that first Christian Pentecost. Baptize me anew in your Holy Spirit. Empower me to build your church and your kingdom in this world. Amen.

Notes

1. Edwin Hatch, "Breathe on me, Breath of God," adapted by Anthony G. Petti, *New Catholic Hymnal* (London: Faber Music Ltd., 1970). Used with permission.

2. *The Holy Spirit, Growth of a Biblical Tradition* (originally published by Paulist Press in 1976, reprinted by Hendrickson, and now available from Wipf & Stock Publishers), 64–68.

3. *Targum Neofiti* 1, I on Genesis 1:2).

4. Pope John Paul II, *Dominum et Vivificantem*, May 18, 1986, 41.

5. *De Decalogo*, 32–35.

6. Joni Mitchell, "Both Sides Now."

7. Pope John Paul II, *Mother of the Redeemer*, March 25, 1987, 44.

8. *The Gift of Prophecy, The Word of Knowledge, The Gift of Tongues, Resting in the Spirit* and many books on healing. See the complete list at www.degrandisssj.com.

9. St. Hilary, *De Baptismo*, 20.

10. A. R. Jain, "My Body, Jain Bodies, and the Denigration of the Body: Self-Reflexivity and the Analysis of the Body in the Jain Tradition," *Council of Societies for the Study of Religion Bulletin* 36 (April 2007), 49.

11. Ibid., 51.

12. Pope Paul VI, *Evangelii Nuntiandi*, December 8, 1975, 41.

13. William Shakespeare, *The Merchant of Venice*, Act I, Scene III.

14. This is my translation of the Greek. The text echoes the tradition by attributing creation to the spirit of the Lord and his word (voice).

15. St. Ignatius of Antioch, *Letter to the Romans*, introduction. The expression can also be translated "presiding over love (*agape*)," and in that sense, if love stands for the universal church, it would be an early affirmation of the primacy of the church of Rome.